I0518488

CHRISTA PIERCE

Adulting 101

Things I Wish I Knew Before I Moved Out My Momma's House

SOLOMON'S PEN
PUBLISHING

First published by Solomon's Pen Publishing 2025

Copyright © 2025 by Christa Pierce

All rights reserved. No part of this publication may be reproduced, stored or transmitted in any form or by any means, electronic, mechanical, photocopying, recording, scanning, or otherwise without written permission from the publisher. It is illegal to copy this book, post it to a website, or distribute it by any other means without permission.

Library of Congress Control Number: 2025920003

First edition

ISBN: 979-8-9996820-0-0

This book is a heartfelt dedication to my beloved daughter, Tyler. With the wisdom and talent contained within these pages, I hope to empower you to overcome the financial challenges that have plagued our family for generations and pave the way for the creation of lasting wealth. TyTy, your potential knows no bounds, and I cherish you more than words can express.

"Nobody hands you a manual when you move out on your own. This book is the manual I wish I had, real talk, real lessons, and a few bumps and bruises along the way, so maybe you don't have to earn yours the hard way."

- Christa Pierce

Contents

Preface

When I stepped out into the "real world" for the first time, I thought adulthood would feel like freedom, late nights, cute apartments, money in the bank, and a life straight out of a rom-com movie. Nobody mentioned the part where adulthood is really just juggling bills, credit scores, paying taxes, making daily life decisions, and trying not to cry in the shower when the days get really tough.

And here's the truth: **Most young adults are being thrown into life wildly unprepared, and it's not their fault.** We grew up memorizing dates from history books and solving equations we'd never use again, but no one pulled us aside and said:

- This is how credit really works.
- This is why you have to pay taxes.
- This is how you budget and save for your future.
- This is how to choose a career path, not just a major.
- This is how to take care of yourself mentally, financially, and emotionally.

I wrote this book because I didn't have a guide when I needed one. I learned many things the hard way through mistakes, stress, Google searches at 2 a.m., and wishing somebody had prepared me better.

Young adults entering into adulthood deserve better than

being dropped into the world with nothing but "good luck." This book is the manual I wish someone had handed me before I moved out.

A survival guide.

A blueprint.

A real-talk coach in paperback form.

If you're stepping into adulthood, or you're already knee-deep in it, trying to figure it out, this book is for you. You don't have to guess your way through life. You don't have to struggle to "figure it out eventually." You deserve knowledge, direction, and support from the start.

Welcome to adulthood, the honest version.

Let's navigate this thing called life together.

Christa Pierce

Acknowledgments

First and foremost, I want to thank God because without God, I wouldn't be able to do any of this. Next, I want to thank my daughter, Tyler, and her friends. Without them constantly asking me questions about life, I wouldn't have thought to write this much-needed book, as most young adults are going out into the adult world ill-prepared.

I want to express my deepest gratitude to my incredible family. Your unwavering support and belief in my vision have been the foundation of this journey. To my mom, thank you for your endless encouragement and for always pushing me to reach my potential. Your love and guidance have been my greatest source of strength.

To my friends, thank you for standing by me through every challenge and celebrating every milestone. Your faith in me and my work has been truly inspiring. You have been my cheerleaders, confidants, and sounding boards, and I am forever grateful for your presence in my life. Thank you to everyone who shared their own experiences and wisdom with me along the way. Your insights have enriched this book and made it what it is today.

Finally, to all the readers embarking on your own journey of adulting, I hope this book serves as a helpful guide and source of encouragement. Thank you for allowing me to be a part of your adventure.

Introduction

If you're holding this book, that probably means you're either *about* to move out on your own or you already did, and life hit you like a ton of bricks that dropped out of the sky. Either way, welcome to the hood, adulthood that is. It's giving freedom, yes, but also bills, responsibilities, and a whole lot of "what the heck am I doing?"

Let me tell you, when I first moved out of my momma's house, I *thought* I had it all figured out. Sis was feelin' grown. I had my own keys to a little apartment and no curfew. I was living! Until it was time to cook a real meal, unclog a toilet, or figure out why my bank account was playing peek-a-boo with my direct deposit.

This book is my "child, let me put you on" moment. It's full of all the lessons I learned the *hard* way, mixed with some advice, hacks, and "don't be like me" tips to help you not just survive out here but actually thrive.

We're going to talk money (because being broke is not cute), saving for the future (yes, you need a retirement plan even if you're still in your twenties), adult friendships and networking (aka making friends who know a good mechanic), and keeping your peace (because adulting will test you). Oh, and yes, we'll cover taxes. Don't roll your eyes, it's important.

Each chapter is straight to the point, easy to digest, and sprinkled with my personal tea, so you don't feel like you're reading a boring textbook. My goal is to help you feel a little more prepared and a lot less overwhelmed as you step into this next phase of life.

So, whether you're just packing your bags to leave the nest or you've already flown the coop and are wondering if you should fly back, this book is for you. We're doing this together, okay?

So, let's get started, and may your coffee be strong, your bills be on autopay, and adulthood feel just a little less chaotic from here on out.

1

Adulting Isn't All It's Cracked Up to Be

Welcome to Adulthood!

"*I can't wait to grow up.*"

I used to say that all the time as a kid, probably while staring dramatically out the window like I was in some coming-of-age movie. I just *knew* adulthood was going to be lit, no bedtime, eating cookies for breakfast if I felt like it, wearing what I wanted, going wherever I wanted without having to ask my momma first. She made it all look so easy and glamorous, like she had it all figured out. Spoiler alert: she didn't. And now that I'm grown, I laugh every time I think about how pressed I was to be an adult.

Because here's the truth nobody tells you: being a grown-up is extremely hard sometimes. When you're a kid, your biggest dilemma is picking the perfect first day of school outfit or figuring out who you're sitting with at lunch. Then boom, you grow up, and suddenly you're juggling bills, trying to stretch a paycheck, Googling how to do your taxes, and realizing laundry is a *never-ending* situation. And let's not even talk about cooking every single day and still having to wash dishes afterwards. Who signed us up for this?

The Freedom Checklist

The freedom we couldn't wait for as kids comes with a whole checklist of responsibilities. Sure, you *can* stay up all night binge-watching Netflix. But guess who still has to get up for work at 7 a.m.? (Hint: it's you. Tired, crusty, and full of regrets.)

Now, don't get me wrong, there *are* perks to being grown. You can make your own rules, travel when you want, decorate your place how *you* like, and start building the life you always dreamed about. But let's be real: adulthood is basically a full-time job with no days off. You're responsible for *everything*. Your choices, your money, your peace, your future, all on you. And some days it feels like a juggling act with no training wheels.

Pay Attention, Rookie

If you're still in your teens, listen, soak it *all* in. Enjoy not paying rent. Enjoy that refrigerator full of food you didn't have to buy. Enjoy taking naps like it's a sport. Because once you cross over into grown-up land, it's game on. There's no looking back, just you, your responsibilities, and the slow realization that being a kid was the real dream.

Smoney: My Biggest Adulting Struggle

Now, let me keep it all the way real for a second. Do you know one of the biggest things I struggled with growing up? Money. Nobody ever sat me down and said, "Hey girl, let me show you how this credit thing works." Not my momma, not my grandmother. Money problems felt like a family curse growing up. The only person who broke the cycle was my uncle, who learned from my grandmother's mistakes and flipped the script. But I had to learn the hard (and expensive) way.

The Credit Card Wake-Up Call

At 19, I got my first credit card, and I thought I hit the jackpot. Swipe, swipe, swipe! Shopping like I was rich when I barely had gas money. I didn't know a thing about interest, due dates, or that paying late could have your credit score looking like a bad test grade. It took me *years* to clean that mess up. Looking back, I wish someone had just explained how important credit really is. But honestly, how could my momma teach me something she never learned herself?

Listen, adulting is no joke. But the good news is, you don't have to have it all figured out today. This is your time to learn, grow, and glow up. You'll mess up (we all do), but you'll also discover just how resilient and capable you really are.

Do you know one of the biggest lessons I've learned? *Credit is everything, more so than money.* It's not just a number, it's a whole key to life. It can open doors, or it can lock them. But before we even get to the credit part, we have to start with the basics: your bank account. We'll get to that in a minute.

Next Stop: College or Certification?

Before you start dreaming about your first big paycheck, you've got to decide how you're actually going to get into your career. Are you going to college? Or do you see a certification in your future? Or do you skip the classroom drama entirely and dive straight into the workforce? In the next chapter, we'll break down the pros, the cons, the dollars, and the sense of each path, so you can choose the route that actually sets you up for success without selling your soul in the process. It's time to make a move, kid.

Why Rap Lyrics Matter

But before we get too deep, let me put you on to something. You'll notice each chapter in this book is named after a rap lyric. That's not by accident. Rap has always been more than just beats and bars; it's a blueprint. A whole masterclass in survival, hustle, confidence, and financial literacy (even if it's wrapped in designer flexes and metaphors). From Jay-Z dropping gems about credit to Drake speaking on growth, loyalty, and securing the bag. Hip-hop has always taught life lessons; we just had to listen beyond the beat.

These lyrics aren't just catchy lines; they're real talk, life lessons disguised as bangers. So I'm using those lyrics to set the tone for each chapter, because they reflect the real-life grown-up stuff we all have to deal with: money, credit, careers, adulting fails, and the glow-up that comes after. It's the culture teaching the class. Welcome to the course.

2

"She Has No Idea What She Doin' In College, That Major That She Majored In Don't Make No Money, But She Won't Drop Out Her Parents 'll Look At Her Funny" ~ Kanye West

To Degree or Not to Degree? That Is the Question

In the song *All Falls Down*, Kanye West calls out a reality a lot of people don't like to admit: many students end up in college without a clear plan, committed to majors that don't lead to financial stability, but afraid to switch directions because of family expectations. And that's real life. A lot of young adults don't stay in school because it's the best option for them; they stay because walking away feels like failure, and disappointing others feels worse.

This chapter is about cutting through that pressure and helping you make a thoughtful, informed decision instead of an emotional one, so you can choose a path that actually aligns with your goals, your lifestyle, and your future bank account.

Should You Go to College?

Deciding what to do after high school can feel like standing at a major crossroads with no map, no GPS, and a phone on 3% battery. Do you go to college? Is it really worth the money, the loans, and the stress? Or do you skip it, get a certification, and jump straight into the workforce to start "securing the bag"?

Let's be honest: college isn't for everybody, and that's perfectly okay. Some careers require a degree; think teachers, doctors, lawyers, and engineers. You can't exactly YouTube your way through med school (please don't try). But plenty of high-paying, fulfilling careers don't require a four-year degree. Some tech jobs, digital marketing, design, and skilled trades are wide open to folks who never set foot on a college campus.

When College Makes Sense

If you're still trying to figure out what you want to do with your life (join the club), college can give you time to explore. But if you're going just because your parents, guidance counselor, or that one auntie said you should—pause. Going into debt to "find yourself" isn't ideal. Trust me when I tell you: Sallie Mae doesn't care that you were confused about which road in life to take.

8

If You Choose College, Choose the Right College

Now, if you do decide college is your move, don't just fall for the first school that slides into your inbox like, "Hey, bestie, apply now!" Be strategic. Think about whether you actually like the school or just its football team. This is your future, not a TikTok trend; make it count.

Factors to Consider

Choose a college based on a few important factors:

- Affordability: Can you actually afford to attend?
- **Programs:** Do they have majors that match your interests?
- **Location:** Close to home or far away? City or rural?
- **Total Cost:** Consider tuition, housing, food, and books.
- **Size:** Do you want a small college or a large university?
- **Support Services:** Look for tutoring, mental health resources, and career counseling.

Also, check their graduation rates and job placement stats. A college that helps students graduate and get jobs after school is the place you want to be.

College Without Selling Your Soul (or Your Kidney)

College can be a massive financial burden. You'll find yourself asking, "Why is this textbook $300 when it could've been a free online version?" But here's the good news: it doesn't have to drain your bank account or leave you living off ramen noodles for four years straight. With a little planning, you can get a solid education without selling a kidney on the black market (kidding... mostly).

Take AP or Dual-Enrollment Classes in High School for College Credit

High school can double as college prep if you play it right. AP and dual-enrollment classes let you earn college credits early. You can skip some courses later and maybe even graduate sooner. It's like fast-forwarding through the boring parts. Bonus: your future self will thank you for not having to take "Intro to Stuff" twice.

Apply for Grants and Scholarships Early and Often

Grants and scholarships are like free money that magically appears if you actually apply for them. You want to know the secret to getting grants and scholarships? Start early and don't be shy. Apply to *all* of them.

There are scholarships for everything from academic achievements to weird hobbies you didn't even know you had. Also, fill out your FAFSA as soon as it opens. Think of it like getting in line early for concert tickets, except the concert is "not drowning in student debt."

In many states, you can apply for scholarships directly from your state legislators, your State Senator, and State Representatives (or Delegates, depending on the state). These legislative scholarships are awarded to residents in their districts who are attending college or career schools, and the amounts can range from a few hundred dollars to several thousand. The process usually requires you to file your FAFSA by your state's deadline and then contact your legislators' offices to request the application. Because each legislator offers their own scholarship, applying to all of them can increase your chances of getting more aid. It's a lesser-known resource that students in many states overlook, but it can be one of the easiest ways to secure extra funding for school.

Start at a Community College, Then Transfer to a University

Why pay the full price right away when you can ease into college life cheaply? Community colleges are basically the budget-friendly starter pack for your degree. You knock out your general education requirements without selling that kidney. After two years, you can transfer to a university and finish up. Colleges love transfer students, by then you've finally retired from your "professional major hopper" era and sorta-kinda know what you want to do with your life.

Look Into In-State Public Schools for Lower Tuition

Out-of-state schools might sound glamorous until you see the price tag. Staying in-state often means paying way less because the government's basically pitching in to keep you close. Plus, many state schools have great programs and social scenes.

So you don't have to miss out on the full college experience. Living on campus can still give you that "I'm an adult" feeling while keeping you close enough to drive to mom's for Sunday dinner.

Live Off-Campus with Roommates to Save on Housing

Dorms might be convenient, but they also cost a pretty penny. Sharing a place off-campus with roommates is like splitting the bill for life, and it can save you tons. Just remember: pick roommates wisely or you'll be paying rent AND therapy bills. Also, scouting less trendy neighborhoods can be your wallet's best friend.

Cook Your Own Meals Instead of Eating Out

Yes, college ramen is a thing, but cooking your own meals saves you way more money (and probably your stomach). Buy staples like pasta and rice, prep meals ahead of time, and suddenly you're a kitchen ninja. Plus, you'll avoid the "oops, I spent my whole paycheck on Uber Eats" surprise.

Take Advantage of Campus Resources

Your university is basically handing out freebies: free bus passes, free concerts, free counseling, free career advice. Use 'em! Why pay for entertainment or health care when your campus probably already has it? Treat the career center like your new best friend; internships found there can turn into jobs with actual paychecks.

Work Part-Time or Freelance for Extra Cash

You can't just wish money into existence, unfortunately. Working part-time on or near campus helps cover bills, and freelance gigs let you flex any skills you have, writing, design, tutoring, you name it. Plus, a job looks good on your resume.

Don't Major in Broke

College is expensive, and student loans are no joke. So many people go to school for 4+ years, rack up thousands (even hundreds of thousands) in debt, and graduate into a field that barely pays enough to cover rent—let alone loan payments. Don't do that to yourself.

Going to college for four years and getting a degree that costs you $100,000 in tuition, just to graduate and get a job barely making $50,000 a year, is hustling backward. Passion is important, but so is having a roof over your head and not crying when Sallie Mae comes knocking. You've got to find the balance between what you enjoy and what will pay off in the long run. And the truth is, there are plenty of high-paying careers that still let you pursue your interests, but you've got to look ahead and be smart about it.

If you're going to spend 4+ years in school and tens of thousands of dollars, make sure you're walking into a career with real earning potential right out of college. Look into fields like tech, healthcare, finance, and skilled trades, industries that are growing, paying well, and won't leave you living paycheck to paycheck.

Careers: Where Reality Smacks Passion in the Face

Picking a career isn't just about doing what you love; it's about doing what will pay your bills, build your future, and help you live a life that's not just financially stable but fulfilling too.

You've got to be strategic when planning a career. That means considering your interests and skills, but also looking at the numbers: job demand, starting salary, growth opportunities, and how much debt you'll have to take on to get there.

Questions to Ask Yourself

- What am I naturally good at?
- How much money do I need to live the life I want?
- What kind of work makes me feel motivated or excited, even if I'm not getting paid (yet)?

Then look at careers that match up with those answers, but don't stop there. Check the job outlook, average starting salary, and how long (and how expensive) the education or training will be. Because "fun" won't pay the rent, but a smart career choice can pay for both rent *and* the vacation you'll need after working it.

Big Bucks, No Grad School Required

Nobody I know wakes up saying, "Yes, please, sign me up for seven years of college and crushing debt. But I did it, four years undergrad, two years grad school, and a whole lot of torture sprinkled in. If I had known there were easier ways to make good money without the endless lectures and overpriced textbooks, you better believe I would've saved myself time, money, and a few gray hairs. These careers listed below pay well, actually have a future, and don't require you to sacrifice your twenties in a classroom.

With a 4-Year Degree

- **Software Developer** – Coding is the new literacy. High demand, high pay.
- **Data Analyst** – If you're good with numbers and like solving problems, this field is probably for you.
- **Cybersecurity Analyst** – Digital bodyguard of the 21st century. With cyber threats everywhere, companies pay well to keep hackers out of their systems. Certifications often matter more than degrees here.
- **Machine Learning Engineer (A.I.)** – The brains behind self-driving cars, chatbots, and recommendation engines. This role builds algorithms that help machines "learn" and is one of the fastest-growing, best-paid fields in tech.
- **A.I. Prompt Engineer** – The new kid on the block. Specialists who know how to "talk" to A.I. tools to get the best results—mixing creativity with technical know-how. Salaries are climbing fast as businesses scramble to integrate A.I. into everything.
- **Registered Nurse (RN)** – Always in demand, especially with an aging population. Flexible career paths and solid pay make nursing a dependable choice.
- **Radiology Nurse** – The healthcare pro who works alongside doctors and techs during diagnostic imaging and radiation treatments. They combine nursing skills with tech know-how, making them key players in hospitals and clinics. Solid pay, strong demand, and plenty of room to specialize.
- **Cloud Engineer** – The backbone of modern businesses. Cloud engineers design and maintain the systems that let companies run everything online. High demand and even higher salaries.

- **Marketing Manager** – Ideal for those who are creative and analytical, turning ideas into campaigns that drive sales.
- **Financial Analyst** – Help people or companies grow their money by making smart investments and budgeting decisions.
- **Industrial Engineer** – Focused on systems, efficiency, and improving processes across industries.

Don't go shutting down whole career fields with, "I don't like tech." Chill. Tech isn't just coding in a dark basement while living off Red Bull. There are niches. Maybe you're artsy, obsessed with colors, fonts, and making things look good, boom, that's UX/UI or user experience/user interface design.

And don't side-eye the whole medical field just because you're not about that Grey's Anatomy life, elbow-deep in somebody's chest cavity. Not every job requires eight years of med school and a pager that never stops. Maybe you're squeamish, but organized medical billing or health admin could be right up your alley. Maybe you like people, but not, you know, their insides. Try physical therapy or nursing support. The point is, there are lanes in medicine that don't involve scalpels or blood splatter on your sneakers. So instead of tossing the whole industry in the trash, find the corner of it that actually matches your vibe.

Certifications 101: Your Fast Track to the Bag

So you looked at college, saw the price tag, and said, "I'll pass," and now you're eyeing certifications. Smart move on so many levels. Certifications can actually do the thing college promises: get you a job, without making you sell a kidney or live on ramen noodles for four years. They're faster, cheaper, and usually don't come with professors who "forget" to reply to your emails when you have a question about that dreaded group project.

Basically, certifications are like receipts that say, "Yeah, I actually know what I'm doing." You can earn them through boot camps, workshops, or specialized programs; they cover everything from coding to medical billing to Project Management Professional (PMP). In short, they open doors to jobs that pay really good money out of the gate. Here's why certifications might just be your new best adulting hack:

Clock In Yesterday: Fast-Track Your Career

The best part about certifications? You don't have to spend four years pretending to figure out life while maxing out your parents' credit card. Many programs can be finished in just a few weeks to a few months, so you can actually start earning money before your college classmates are halfway through their second semester.

Coding bootcamps take about 8–12 weeks, and you could be typing your way into a tech job. With a Google IT Support certification in six months, you might already be getting paid to fix other people's computer problems. In short: learn the skills, get the paycheck, skip the dorm drama. Your future self and your bank account will thank you.

Keep Your Wallet Happy: Cheap Credentials That Actually Work

College tuition got you clutching your pearls? Yeah, we feel you. Enter certifications: the budget-friendly way to actually learn something useful without selling a kidney to pay for it. Most programs cost a tiny fraction of a degree, and many even let you pay in installments, so you're not crying over a giant bill before your first paycheck.

Want proof? A medical billing or coding certification might set you back a few hundred bucks—or a couple thousand if you want to go fancy. Compare that to tens of thousands for a traditional degree, and suddenly your bank account is doing a happy dance. Bottom line: you can upskill, get paid, and still have money left for avocado toast.

No Degree? No Problem. Skills Pay the Bills.

Not every high-paying gig cares about a fancy degree. Some industries actually value what you can *do* over what some college gave you in a folder. That's where certifications, apprenticeships, and trade schools swoop in like superheroes.

Plumbing? Welding? Project management? IT support? Yup, all fair game without a four-year degree. These fields want someone who can handle the work, not someone who can memorize a syllabus. These fields prove you've got the hands-on skills to get the job done, and sometimes even better than the degree hanging on your wall.

Learn the Art of the Pivot!

You're never locked into one job. Any day you can wake up and decide you want a new career. If you're looking to switch careers, certifications offer a practical and effective way to gain the necessary skills in a new field without starting from scratch. Whether you want to move into tech, healthcare, or business management, certifications can provide the specialized knowledge you need to make a career transition smoothly.

My Story: How I Doubled My Income by Betting on Myself

Let me put you on to a career pivot that didn't just change my title, it changed my life *and* my bank account.

I spent a few years working at a nonprofit, and they call it "nonprofit" for a reason, because the profit was *nonexistent* in my paycheck. I was making "save the world" money, not "upgrade to first class" money. My salary hovered around $65K a year, which sounds like a lot–until you realize it doesn't go far if you're trying to live a little. My goal was to travel four times a year, but how could I on that salary? I was lucky to squeeze in one and a half. And when raise season came around, it was always the same speech: *"We're not in this to get rich, we're here to make a difference."* Cool... but my bank account was out here making a whole different kind of statement.

The funniest part was hearing that from a CEO pulling in a $2 million a year salary. Like, Sir, trust, I want to make a difference too...preferably in my checking account.

I couldn't help feeling like I had more in me and more to earn. Meanwhile, I had this passion on the side: web design. I'd taught myself HTML, CSS, JavaScript, and WordPress with nothing but grit, YouTube, and Codecademy. I was designing and building websites as a freelancer, but I didn't feel like a "real" designer, just a side hustler with a laptop and a dream.

Although I had a college degree and had taken some design courses in school, I didn't have a degree in web design. I let that fear hold me back from applying to roles I knew I could excel in. I thought I needed a traditional degree to be taken seriously in the tech design world.

Then I discovered the Google UX Design Professional Certificate through the Grow with Google program. It was affordable, flexible, and best of all, designed for people like me who had skills but needed the confidence (and credentials) to back it up.

I committed to it. I studied evenings and weekends. I built a portfolio. I learned the UX/UI lingo and began to see how my web design background and project experience actually fit perfectly into this field.

Three months after completing the certification, I landed my first full-time UX/UI designer job, and my salary jumped from $65K to over $100K.

All because I took a chance on myself. I stopped waiting to be "qualified" and started showing that I was. The certification didn't just teach me new skills; it validated the knowledge I already had and gave me the confidence to own my value.

What You Can Learn from My Journey & Break Into Tech the Easy Way

Honestly, times have changed, and you don't need a fancy degree to get started. Real-world skills and a solid portfolio can open doors, especially in tech. Certifications aren't just paper; they boost your credibility, show employers you're serious, and prove you can deliver. And if you're self-taught? Don't sleep on that. Your experience already has value, classroom or not.

Want to level up without dropping thousands? Here's the cheat sheet I used to teach myself new skills for free or basically free, so you can become a legit pro in whatever tech or non-tech area you're curious about:

- *Codecademy, FreeCodeCamp & SheCodes:* Learn to code without selling a kidney. Front-end, back-end, data, you name it, they've got you.
- *Grow with Google:* Not just UX/UI. IT support, cloud computing, data analytics...a buffet of tech skills to see what sticks.
- *YouTube:* Tutorials for days. Build an app, a website, or even teach a robot to do your laundry. There's a video for that.
- *Build a Portfolio:* Even fake projects count. Show the world you can actually do the thing, not just talk about it at family dinners.
- *Freelance or Volunteer:* Get real experience, get paid, and flex your skills helping small businesses, nonprofits, or anyone who'll let you in their tech sandbox.

Job-Ready Tips

- Tailor your resume with keywords from job descriptions.
- Highlight certifications and self-taught projects proudly.
- Don't wait until you "feel ready." Apply anyway. You might surprise yourself.
- If you're already doing the work, don't wait for permission. Get certified, get confident, and go get your bag.

Certifications That Won't Waste Your Life (or Your Money)

Not all certifications are created equal. Some are pure gold in the job market. Some others are expensive paperweights for your wall. The trick is doing your homework before you drop cash or months of your life.

Start by stalking job postings in the field you want to break into. See which certifications employers actually care about: "required" or "preferred." Then tap your network: ask mentors, industry pros, or online communities if a cert is legit. Professional organizations can also clue you in on what's actually worth your time.

And don't sleep on the cost or time commitment. Some certifications are quick, cheap, and open doors faster than you can say "first paycheck." Others take months, cost a fortune, and actually pay off big time too. And then there's the sad category of expensive programs that take forever and won't move the needle. Be smart. Pick a certification that earns you skills, cash, and respect, not just likes on your LinkedIn feed.

Grow with Google: Your Shortcut to Real Skills

If you've ever thought, "I wish I could learn tech stuff without dropping a fortune," say hello to Grow with Google. This is Google's free (or low-cost) learning hub designed to teach real-world skills that employers actually care about. It's like having a tech mentor who doesn't yell at you for asking dumb questions.

What Grow with Google Offers:

1. Courses and Certifications in Multiple Areas

- *IT Support* – Become the go-to person keeping systems running smoothly.
- *Data Analytics* – Learn to interpret numbers and make smart business decisions.
- *Project Management* – Get organized, lead projects, and impress your boss.
- *Cloud Computing* – Understand the tech that runs the internet behind the scenes.
- *UX Design* – Build websites and apps people actually love to use.

2. Flexible Learning: Most programs are online, self-paced, and affordable—some are completely free. You can study evenings, weekends, or whenever you've got a quiet moment between TikTok binges.

3. Real-World Skills That Get You Hired: Courses aren't just theory—they include hands-on projects and assignments you can put directly in your portfolio. By the time you finish, you've got something tangible to show employers: proof you can actually do the work.

4. Career Resources: Google doesn't just hand you a certificate and say, "Good luck." They provide resume tips, interview prep, and guidance on landing entry-level jobs in your chosen field. It's like having a little career GPS guiding you to your first paycheck.

5. Accessible for Everyone: Whether you're a recent high school grad, a self-taught coder, or someone pivoting careers, Grow with Google is designed to be approachable. No fancy tech jargon required at the start—you learn as you go.

Why It Matters: In today's job market, skills often matter more than degrees. Grow with Google gives you credible, employer-recognized credentials without years of debt or decades of waiting. In other words, it's a fast lane to launching a real career, not just collecting certificates to hang on your wall.

College vs. Certification, Which One's For You?

When it comes to choosing between college and a certification, it really depends on your goals, budget, and timeline. College is the long game—it takes years, costs a pretty penny, and gives you a well-rounded education that can open doors to a wide range of careers (especially in fields where a degree is non-negotiable). A certification, on the other hand, is like a career fast pass—it's cheaper, quicker, and laser-focused on teaching you one specific skill so you can jump right into the job market. If you're looking for broad opportunities and higher long-term earning potential, college might be your lane. But if you want to get in, get skilled, and get paid without spending four years writing papers you'll never look at again, a certification could be the smarter move.

Factors	College Degree	Certification Program
Time	2-4+ years	Weeks to 2 years
Cost	$$$$ (tuition, books, housing)	$-$$$
Flexibility	Less flexible	Often online/self-paced
Job Readiness	Broad, general	Direct, specific skills
Career Options	More long-term options	Fast entry to specific fields

What Happens After College or Certification?

Getting a degree or a certification isn't the finish line—it's just the starting pistol. Whether you're holding a piece of paper from a university or a shiny cert from a bootcamp, now it's time to turn that credential into real-world momentum. Here's how to make the most of it:

- *Start job hunting early:* don't wait until graduation.
- *Get experience:* Internships, apprenticeships, or even volunteering can set you apart from other job seekers.
- *Update your resume and LinkedIn:* Your digital presence matters. Clean it up and ensure it accurately reflects your

skills.

- *Keep learning:* Career paths evolve. You might need new skills or certifications down the line. Be ready and willing to adapt.

Your career isn't just a job, it's a lifestyle. Choose one that supports the life you want to live. You don't have to be rich, but you do need to be financially stable. So, before you drop tens of thousands on a degree, ask yourself: "Will this degree help me earn enough to live the life I want and pay back my student loans?"

Pick smart. Choose fields that are growing. Look for high starting salaries. And most importantly, don't follow the crowd. Follow the money and your passions with your eyes wide open.

Final Thought

Whether you go the college route or choose certifications, the goal is to build a life you enjoy and can afford. Don't pick a path just to make your parents happy or to keep up with your friends. Pick the one that aligns with your vision of success.

The key is this: there's no one right path, just the one that's right for you. Do your homework, ask questions, try things out, and don't be afraid to change directions because it's all about the art of the pivot. You're not stuck, you're just getting started.

3

"Financial Freedom My Only Hope F*ck Living Rich and Dying Broke" ~ Jay-Z

Where the Money Resides: Bank Accounts, Budgeting, and Breaking the Cycle

I n the song *Moment of Clarity*, Jay-Z made it clear that his real goal wasn't about looking rich in the moment, but about building financial security that lasts, and that message only hits harder the older you get. Because a lot of people make good money and still struggle, simply because no one taught them how to manage it. If you don't get a grip on your finances early, it's very possible to still be stressed, confused, and living paycheck to paycheck well into your forties.

And trust me, I didn't come out the womb knowing how to budget. I once thought "balancing a checkbook" was some outdated skill nobody actually used, and I treated overdraft fees like they were just banks being mean and greedy. Plot twist, it wasn't the bank. It was me. This chapter is about learning how to handle your money with intention, so you're not just surviving adulthood, but actually building the kind of financial freedom that gives you options.

Your Bank Account: Your New Best Frenemy

Once upon a time, people stuffed their money under their mattresses as a way to save money. Doing that now is like the financial version of leaving your car running with the doors unlocked. Technically, it might be fine, but why gamble? These days, a real bank account does way more than just hold your money; it keeps it safe, helps you track your spending, and makes managing bills a breeze. Sure, Cash App and Venmo are fine for splitting brunch or sending your cousin gas money, but they're not designed to protect your money long-term, earn interest, or help you build a solid financial history. A legitimate bank account gives you security, reliability, and the paper trail you need for big-life moves like renting an apartment, buying a car, or applying for a loan. So basically, you need a real bank account at a real bank.

Here's why you need one:

- Safe & Sound – FDIC insurance covers your money up to $250,000, better protection than your cousin guarding your Netflix password.
- Swipe, Don't Hide – Debit cards, apps, and ATMs mean you don't have to carry a bag full of singles.
- Money Detective Mode – See exactly where your cash is going, yes, even those $6 Starbucks runs.
- Direct Deposit = Fast Money – Your paycheck hits your account like magic.

- Builds Street Cred – Need an apartment or a loan? A bank account shows you're legit adulting.

Picking a Bank That Doesn't Rob You Blind

Not all banks play nice. Some act like they're doing you a favor by holding your money hostage, charging you for every little thing, like it's 1999. Others *want* your business and make life easier. The trick is knowing the difference before you sign on the dotted line. A good bank should feel like a teammate, not a scammy ex who drains your account when you're not looking.

And don't sleep on credit unions, either. Places like Navy Federal or local community credit unions often offer better rates and lower fees than the big banks. Plus, you can usually join if a family member already has an account, so it's kind of like a money hookup through your relatives. So ask around and see if any of your family members have the hook-up.

What to Look For in a Bank

Here's what to keep an eye out for when you're choosing where to house your hard-earned money:

- *No Monthly Fees* – Or at least ones that vanish if you set up direct deposit. Because why should you pay to access your own money?
- *Nearby ATMs* – Trust me, nothing stings like paying $3 every time you need $20. That's basically an instant 15% "I'm broke" tax.
- *Apps That Work* – You shouldn't need Wi-Fi, three prayers, and a tech degree just to check your balance. Look for

smooth bill pay, mobile deposits, and instant balance checks.

- *Customer Service That Answers* – Because sitting on hold for two hours listening to elevator music while your money is missing is pure torture.

Checking vs. Savings: What's the Deal?

You need both a checking and a savings account because they play two totally different roles in your money game. One keeps your everyday life running, the other makes sure your future self isn't broke and stressed. Think of them as teammates; you can't win the game with just one.

Checking: Your Financial Playground

Think of a checking account as your financial playground. That's where your paycheck drops, bills get snatched up, and those "I deserve it" impulse buys slide through without hesitation. It's built for constant swiping, paying, and moving money around, basically, your day-to-day money hustle.

Savings: Your Grown-Up Stash Spot

A savings account, though? That's your grown-up stash spot. It's not for instant gratification, it's for the long game. This is where your rainy-day fund, emergency stash, or "I'm finally taking that trip" money lives. You don't touch it every day, and if you're smart, you let it sit and grow with interest, slow and steady. And here's the kicker: you don't have to stop at just one savings account. A lot of people set up multiple savings "buckets" for different goals, like one for emergencies, one for vacations, and one just to crush Christmas shopping without maxing out your credit card. Having separate accounts makes it way easier to stay disciplined and not "accidentally" spend your future vacation money on late-night DoorDash.

How to Open a Bank Account: Easier Than Assembling IKEA Furniture

Opening a bank account is one of the easiest adulting wins you can score. It's quick, straightforward, and gives you the foundation to actually manage your money instead of stuffing it in your sock drawer. Most banks and credit unions make the process painless; you just need to show up prepared.

Here's what you'll typically need:

- *A valid ID* — Driver's license, state ID, or passport. They just need to know you are who you say you are.
- *Proof of address* — A utility bill, lease agreement, or even official mail with your name and address works. Basically, they want to know you're a real person with an actual place to live.
- *A small opening deposit* — Many banks require a minimum deposit, usually around $25, to get your account started. (Some even let you open with $0 if you set up direct deposit—worth asking about.)
- *Your email and phone number* — So they can set up your account, send you updates, and call if something looks suspicious.

Once you've got these in hand, the rest is smooth sailing. You can either walk into a branch and let someone guide you through it, or skip the line and open your account online. When it comes to opening a checking account in person, it can be helpful if you want to ask questions, get guidance from a banker, or set up multiple accounts at once. Online applications are usually faster and let you compare banks without leaving your house, plus some online-only banks offer lower fees or higher interest rates. You'll fill out a few forms, sign your name a couple of times, and boom, you've got an account.

In less than an hour, you'll have a safe place to keep your money, pay your bills, and start building financial habits that actually make life easier. It's the kind of simple step that sets you up for all the bigger money moves down the road.

. Either way, pay attention to the fine print:

- Look out for monthly maintenance fees (and see if they can be waived with direct deposit)
- Overdraft fees (consider overdraft protection or budget apps to stay on track)
- ATM fees (stick to your bank's ATMs or ones that refund fees)
- Paper statement fees are charged for receiving your account statements by mail. Going digital is usually free, faster, and more secure, letting you access and search your statements anytime while saving money.
- Also, be careful not to "abuse" your account; banks can close your account if you have too many overdrafts or repeatedly dispute legitimate charges. Staying on top of your balance and keeping transactions honest not only protects your account but also keeps your banking record in good standing.

Choosing the right account upfront can save you headaches and unnecessary charges down the road.

The "Why Am I Broke?" Prevention Plan

If you don't know where your money's going, congratulations, you're basically letting it run away to join the circus. Your bank's app is your first line of defense. It's like that friend who always screenshots the receipts so nobody can lie about what they paid for.

Make the App Work for You

- Check your balance before swiping. Saves you from that "card declined" walk of shame at Target.
- Slide leftover money from your paycheck into savings before Amazon or DoorDash steals it.
- Deposit checks from your sofa. Just snap a pic, no waiting in line behind somebody paying their bills in quarters.
- Automate your bills so they're paid even if you're binge-watching and forget what day it is.
- Turn on alerts so your bank snitches when your balance is low or money's leaving your account. You should turn on text and email instant transaction alerts.

Additional Apps That Can Help

But don't stop there. If you really want to level up your money game, the apps listed below can back you up, helping you save smarter, budget better, and keep your finances on track:

- Rocket Money – Hunts down subscriptions you didn't even remember signing up for and cancels them.
- Monarch – For people who want to track every dime like a jealous ex.
- NerdWallet – Credit score nerds, this is your playground.
- TimelyBills – Keeps your bills on time so you're not living by candlelight.

And if you're old-school like me, bust out a spreadsheet. The image below shows a sample of the spreadsheet I use in Google Sheets to track my monthly bills. Since I get paid every other week, I split my larger bills, like rent, in half and pay portions each pay period. This strategy helps me stay on top of expenses without draining my entire paycheck at once. By aligning your bills with your paydays, you can avoid being broke before payday #2 and keep your finances balanced instead of chaotic.

Monthly bills					
Household Expenses					
Account	Bill Due Date	Amount Due	1st paycheck	2nd paycheck	Balance Due
Rent	1st	$1,500.00	750.00	$750.00	$0.00
Gas Bill	6th	$39.00	19.50	$19.50	$0.00
Electric Bill	2nd	$60.00	30.00		$30.00
Internet	28th	$50.00	25.00		$25.00
Netflix	30th	$17.99		$17.99	$0.00
Hulu	8th	$9.99			$9.99
Cellphone Bill	15th	$100.00	50.00		$50.00
Car Insurance	15th	$120.00	60.00		$60.00
life Insurance	9th	$21.00		$21.00	$0.00
Mastercard	21st	$250.00			$250.00
Capital One Credit	19th	$0.00			$0.00
Total Expenses		$2,167.98	$934.50	$808.49	$424.99

Build a Budget That Doesn't Suck

Budgeting doesn't have to feel like financial jail. The 50/30/20 rule is a simple way to get started without feeling like you can't enjoy your money. Here's the breakdown: fifty percent of your income goes to needs like rent, groceries, and keeping the lights on. Thirty percent is for wants, yes, that includes your Netflix subscription, your takeout habit, and the occasional impulse buy (hello sneakers). The final twenty percent goes toward savings and debt, like building an emergency fund, stacking retirement coins, or finally tackling that credit card balance you swear you didn't max out. Stick to this formula, and it becomes easier, and you might even start to like it.

Emergency Fund = Your New Bestie

Life will always throw you curveballs; your car may break down, you might get sick, or God forbid, you lose your job. Having 6-12 months of expenses stashed away keeps you from living off credit cards, begging your friends for help, or setting up a GoFundMe to get by in life during your troubling times.

Start small: $500 to $1,000 is a solid goal. Set up automatic deposits from your paycheck into your savings account or automatic transfers from your checking account to your savings account, so it happens without you even noticing.

Final Thought

Look, nobody's asking you to become the Beyoncé of budgeting overnight. Money management isn't about perfection; it's about progress (and avoiding that "why is my account negative

$3.72?" panic). Set up your bank accounts, keep an eye on where your coins are going, build a budget that doesn't make you cry, and save *something* even if it's just the change from your coffee run. The future you will be forever grateful when you're not dodging overdraft fees or counting down to payday like it's a holiday. You got this, kinda.

4

"I'm Not a Businessman, I'm a Business Man!" ~ Jay-Z

Retirement: Setting Up Future-You for a Soft Life

I n the song *Diamonds From Sierra Leone (Remix)*, Jay-Z made it clear that real wealth isn't just about earning money—it's about treating yourself like an investment. That mindset is exactly what retirement planning is about. You're not just working for a paycheck; you're building something designed to take care of you long after you're done working.

Now, before you panic, no, you don't have to become a Wall Street expert or spend your nights reading finance blogs. This isn't about day trading or getting rich overnight. It's about understanding your 401(k), taking advantage of the free money your job is offering through matching, and letting time and compound interest do the heavy lifting. Think of it as setting up a system that works for you while you're busy living your life. Do your part now, so future-you can actually relax, sip cocktails, and enjoy life without stressing over bills or grocery prices. Your twenty-something self might roll their eyes at this chapter, but trust me, your sixty-five-year-old self will thank you later.

401(k) – Your Cheat Code

What is a 401(k) anyway, you're probably asking. A 401(k) is your employer's retirement savings plan. Think of it like a cheat code: save money before taxes, invest in your future, and lower your taxable income all at once. It's basically the government saying, "Hey, you want to adult responsibly? Here's a little help."

Your paycheck portion gets invested in stocks, bonds, mutual funds, or whatever your plan offers. This isn't just money sitting in a jar under your bed—it's actively working for you. And if your employer is halfway decent, they'll match part of it. Free money for existing. Yes, free money. Not a trick.

Here's the deal: every dollar you invest now is a tiny soldier building your future empire. Miss it, and future-you is left building with cardboard boxes instead of Legos.

Employer Match – The Free Money You're Sleeping On

Employer match = free. Freakin'. Money. Think about it: your boss is literally handing you extra cash for showing up and doing what you already agreed to do. Example: You make $3,000 a month, toss in 6% ($180), and your job throws in another 3% ($90). That's $270 going straight into your retirement fund every month.

Not taking advantage of this is like leaving a Target bag at the register. Why would you? Always contribute enough to grab the full match. And when job hunting, don't just ask, "What's the salary?" Nah—ask, "Y'all got a 401(k)? Do you match? How much?" That perk can be the difference between sipping margaritas at 65 or working at Walmart for sneakers you already bought at 25.

Let me break it down further: a full employer match over 10 years can add up to tens of thousands of dollars—money you didn't even have to sweat for. And if you think, "Eh, I'll catch up later," remember this: catching up later is like trying to sprint with a backpack full of bricks—you can do it, but why make life harder?

Compound Interest – Your Money's Money Making Money

Compounding is where your money starts having babies that have babies. That's right: your cash is basically running a side hustle while you binge Netflix and pretend adulting is easy. The longer it has to work, the bigger the payoff. Think of it like a snowball rolling down a hill—small at first, but give it enough time, and it turns into an avalanche of cash.

Start in your twenties? Even $50 a month turns into something respectable. Start in your thirties? Congratulations, you just left half the bag on the table because time is a savage. Let me hit you with some receipts: $200/month starting at 25 = almost $500K by 65. Same $200/month starting at 35? Just over $200K. Same effort, same grind, but starting late costs you hundreds of thousands. Time literally eats money if you snooze.

And don't think compounding is some magic reserved for math nerds. It works quietly, in the background, while you're living your life—Netflix, TikTok, whatever. Your money is literally out here grinding harder than you are, and all it asks is a little consistency. Even $20/month will grow over decades. Yeah, small potatoes now, but future-you is going to be sipping something strong on a private beach, looking back like, *"Damn, I was smart."*

I get it—life hits. Rent, student loans, Uber Eats runs, emergency dentist bills, car repairs that pop up like unwanted party guests—you get it. And yeah, it might feel impossible to put anything aside when bills are stacking. But here's the kicker: even tossing a little in now is way better than tossing a lot later when your window for compounding has slammed shut. Your money grows silently, relentlessly, while you're figuring out life.

Plus, because 401(k) contributions come straight out of your paycheck pre-tax, you won't even notice the difference. That latte you were about to sip in five minutes? Consider it an investment in your future freedom. Skip one fancy coffee, and boom—you're $50 closer to sipping something stronger in retirement without a single care in the world. It's like adulting with a cheat code, and honestly? Future-you deserves that.

Tax Perks That Hit Different

Traditional 401(k) - Pay Taxes Later

Traditional 401(k) is the "I'll deal with taxes later" vibe. You shove your money into a pre-tax account, which lowers your taxable income right now. Uncle Sam doesn't get his cut until you retire, and if you're lucky, you'll be in a lower tax bracket by then. Translation: more coins stay in your bag today instead of disappearing into the government's pockets. It's basically a discount on adulthood—like finding out your overpriced latte comes with free Wi-Fi and a donut.

The key here is timing. You're deferring taxes so your money has more time to grow before anyone comes knocking. Start early, stay consistent, and your bag could be way fatter than if you waited until your 40s to play this game.

Roth 401(k) - Pay Taxes Upfront

Roth 401(k) flips the script. You pay taxes upfront, meaning no instant thrill—but when you retire? Withdrawals are tax-free. Every penny you take out is yours to spend however you want. Uncle Sam already got his share, so he can take a permanent nap. Think of it like buying a concert ticket months in advance instead of sneaking in later and praying no one notices. Pain now, sweet payoff later.

Roth is especially juicy if you expect to be balling hard in retirement and don't want half your bag gobbled up by taxes. It's the ultimate "set it and forget it" move for your future self, assuming you start now and stick with it.

Which One's Better?

Honestly? It depends. Traditional = tax break now. Roth = tax-free later. Your choice comes down to your current cash flow, income, and how you see your money situation in 20–30 years. Don't guess. Don't ask Reddit. Don't Google at 2 a.m. asking, "Roth or 401(k)?" Talk to someone who actually knows the game—a financial advisor. They get paid to translate all the confusing jargon into plain English, so you don't accidentally shoot yourself in the foot.

And just so we're clear: knowing the difference between Roth and Traditional now isn't just for flexing on your friends. It's literally how you make sure future-you isn't crying into ramen noodles while everyone else is sipping rosé on a beach.

Investment Options – Don't Just Click Default

Options Available

401(k) isn't a piggy bank. You get to pick: stocks, bonds, mutual funds, target-date funds, all that finance jazz. Target-date = lazy-person mode: set your retirement year, fund shifts automatically from risky when young to safe when old. Cruise control, basically.

Target-date funds are the lazy-person move, and honestly, there's nothing wrong with that. You pick your retirement year, and the fund magically shifts from "YOLO-risky" when you're young to "safe and boring" as you get older. It's like cruise control for your money: you don't have to micromanage, but your bag still grows while you live your life.

Risk and Timeline

Here's the deal: your age dictates your vibe. Young and reckless? Cool—take some risks. Stocks can be wild, but you've got decades to recover from the market acting like a toddler on energy drinks.

As you get closer to retirement, you definitely need to chill with the "YOLO investing." You don't need thrills; you need survival. That means safer bets—bonds, stable funds, or low-risk options—so your bag doesn't tank right when you're supposed to be cashing checks and sipping something fancy.

Do Your Homework

Picking investments isn't about flexing on your friends or hoping your money grows magically overnight. It's about making sure future-you isn't scraping by on ramen noodles while everyone else is retired and sipping rosé on a beach.

Do some research. Figure out your comfort level. And yes, talk to an advisor if you're lost. Think of them like a GPS for your money—they know the routes, the traffic, and the shortcuts so your bag gets to its destination in one piece.

Bonus Tip – Don't Sleep on Diversification

Also, don't put all your eggs in one janky basket. Spread your investments around so if one thing tanks, your entire retirement doesn't go up in flames. Stocks, bonds, funds—mix them up. It's like not wearing all your money on one outfit; you want options when life throws curveballs.

Loans and Early Withdrawals – Don't Play Yourself

Look, your 401(k) is supposed to be your retirement stash, not your "oops, I spent too much on brunch and need a bailout" fund. But let's keep it real—life happens. Car breaks down, dentist bills hit like a brick, or you just really, really needed those concert tickets. And suddenly, that pile of cash in your account starts looking like a snack.

Technically, yes, you can borrow from your 401(k). You're just borrowing from yourself, and the money goes right back into your account when you pay it back. Sounds harmless, right? Wrong. There's a catch: you have to pay it back with interest, usually within five years. Fail to do that? Congrats—you just unlocked penalties, taxes, and a front-row seat to financial regret.

And don't even think about taking an early withdrawal. Unless you like paying Uncle Sam a big chunk of your money, leave that cash alone. Anything before 59½ comes with penalties **plus** taxes. Basically, it's like signing up for a financial boot camp you didn't ask for. Painful, unnecessary, and avoidable.

Here's the truth: treating your 401(k) like grandma's fine china is smart. Look at it, admire it, but don't touch it until it's time. Every dollar you leave alone now is a dollar that grows, multiplies, and turns into something future-you can actually enjoy.

When Loans Make Sense

Okay, there are a few legit scenarios where borrowing might work. Emergency medical expenses, preventing eviction, or avoiding high-interest debt like payday loans. Even then, treat it like a last resort. You're still robbing Peter to pay Paul...except Peter is you.

The Long Game

Think of your 401(k) as a plant you can't water too soon. If you pull the roots, it dies. Leave it alone, let it grow, and it becomes a tree that actually feeds you for decades. Every loan or early withdrawal slows that growth. You might get short-term relief, but your long-term bag is steadily shrinking.

Bottom line: hands off unless it's life-or-death. Protect your future self. Future-you isn't going to thank you for popping cash early; they're going to want a fat account, not regrets.

Retirement Isn't Going to Fund Itself

Now, let's get real: your future self sipping something with a mini umbrella on a beach? That's not a gift from the universe. That's the reward for the moves you make today. Investing for retirement isn't just about stashing cash—it's about setting yourself up for freedom, stability, and a life where bills aren't constantly haunting you.

Know Your Options

401(k)s, Roth IRAs, Traditional IRAs, 403(b)s—different accounts come with different perks depending on your job and income. Do your homework. Ignorance isn't bliss—it's a recipe for future-you crying into ramen noodles.

Talk to a Pro

Financial advisors aren't just for rich people or Wall Street bros. They translate the confusing money jargon into plain English, break down your options, and help you make smart moves. Yes, paying someone for advice now beats Googling "401(k) vs. Roth" at 2 a.m. and ending up with regret.

Grab the Free Money

If your job offers a 401(k) match, contributing less than the match is literally leaving money on the table. Take it. Always.

Spread It Out

Multiple accounts = more flexibility and tax perks later. Don't let all your eggs live in one basket, or one market dip could wreck your plans.

Stay in the Know

Rules change. Taxes change. Retirement plans change. Keep up. The last thing you want is to get caught slipping because you thought Social Security would magically cover it all. Spoiler: it won't.

Laugh Now, Cry Later...Or Not

That idyllic "future you on a beach" moment only happens because present-you decided to adult. Don't let fear, confusion, or short-term bills rob you of long-term wealth. Start small, stay consistent, and adjust as life changes.

You're not just saving for retirement—you're buying freedom, peace of mind, and the chance to live life without constantly stressing over money. Future-you deserves better, so make the moves now.

Final Thought

Life's expensive, but you deserve a soft life. Your 401(k) = golden parachute. Don't wait until your knees ache to start. Learn the game, play smart, and future-you will wake up in a paid-off house, see rising debt headlines, and laugh while sipping something with a mini umbrella.

5

"Owe Me Back Like You Owe Your Tax, Owe Me Back Like Forty Acres to Blacks" ~ Nas

Who Is Uncle Sam, and Why Is He Always in My Wallet?

I n his song *You Owe Me*, Nas makes a sharp comparison between owing someone money and owing taxes to drive home one simple truth: taxes are not optional. When he references "forty acres to Blacks," he's pointing to the unfulfilled promise of reparations made to formerly enslaved Black Americans after emancipation, a debt that was promised but never paid. By tying that historical injustice to taxes, Nas is highlighting how the government never forgets what *you* owe, even when it fails to deliver on what it owes others. Uncle Sam isn't your favorite uncle slipping you twenty dollars at a family cookout; he's the U.S. government's alter ego, and he expects his money every time. You can be late on a bill, dodge a call, or "forget" a payment, but owing the government is a different story. Uncle Sam keeps receipts, deadlines, and penalties, and he will always come back for what he's owed.

I get it, the word *taxes* alone makes most people want to crawl under the bed and hide. But understanding how taxes work is one of the smartest adulting moves you can make. This chapter isn't about turning you into a tax expert or making spreadsheets your personality. It's about helping you understand why taxes follow you through every job, side hustle, and paycheck—and how knowing the rules can keep more money in your pocket, and how it will save you from overpaying, stressing, or becoming a cautionary tale on a Netflix doc about tax fraud. So grab a snack, take a deep breath, and let's unpack why Uncle Sam always wants his cut.

So, What Are Taxes Anyway?

Think of taxes as the cover charge for living in America. They're how we pay for government stuff like schools, roads, healthcare, the military, even the pothole you hit every morning that somehow *still* hasn't been fixed. Whether you're buying socks at Target or cashing your paycheck, you're handing Uncle Sam a slice.

The big one you'll care about as a working adult is **Income tax**—a.k.a. the cut taken from the money you bust your butt to earn. Most of the time, your employer plays the middleman and snatches it straight from your paycheck (that's called *withholding*).

But here's the kicker, you still have to file your taxes every year by April 15th—unless the IRS throws us a bone and extends the deadline. Skip it, and they'll hunt you down faster than

Netflix hunts down your password-sharing cousin.

And if you want a taste of reality, just wait for that first paycheck. You'll do the math in your head: "40 hours times $15 an hour = $600." Then you open the envelope (or app) and see $487. Who stole the rest of my money, you'll ask. Surprise! Uncle Sam did, and he didn't even leave a thank-you note.

Your Paycheck: Where Does Your Money Go

Before you even touch a dime, Uncle Sam helps himself to a portion of your paycheck. But understanding where that money's going can actually help you take back some control.

Your paycheck isn't random math your boss pulled out of a hat. Every deduction has a purpose: income taxes, Social Security, Medicare, maybe state taxes (depending on where you live), plus extras like health insurance or retirement contributions if you signed up for them.

Knowing what each line means isn't just adulting trivia—it helps you:

- **Catch errors** (because yes, payroll makes mistakes).
- **Budget smarter** (so you don't spend rent money on sneakers).
- **Plan for refunds** (or avoid that "you owe" surprise come April).

Let's break it down so the next time you look at your pay stub, you'll know exactly why your $600 paycheck turned into $487 before it even hit your account.

List of Different Types of Deductions

Type	What it is
Federal Income Tax	Money taken out based on how much you make and your W-4 info. This goes to the federal government.
State Income Tax	Not all states have this, but if yours does, it's a separate amount paid to the state.
Social Security Tax	6.2% of your paycheck (your employer matches this). Helps fund retirement and disability benefits.
Medicare Tax	1.45% of your paycheck (employer also matches). Pays for healthcare for seniors and people with disabilities.
Local/City Taxes	Some cities or local areas (like NYC or Philly) have their own income taxes.
Other Deductions	Could include health insurance premiums, retirement contributions (like 401(k)), or union dues.

So if your paycheck looks a little slimmer than you imagined, blame the deductions. It stings now, but not all of it is bad news. Some of that money is basically your future-you's savings plan. Things like Social Security and Medicare are deductions you'll tap into once you hit retirement age. And here's the kicker: sometimes you even get a portion back at tax time if your employer withheld more than you actually owed. Think of it like lending Uncle Sam money all year, and then he (hopefully) hands some of it back—minus the interest, of course.

Why Do I Have to File a Tax Return?

Think of your tax return as a yearly check-in with the IRS—a way to make sure you're not accidentally giving them free money or racking up debt. Filing your return shows exactly how much you earned, how much tax has already been taken out, and whether you still owe or are due a refund. It's basically your financial report card: overpaid, and the IRS sends cash back; underpaid, and you get a chance to settle up before the penalties crash the party. Sometimes your job withholds too much (hello, refund), sometimes not enough (hello, bill). Either way, it's on you to file and tell the truth. Stay on top of it, or the IRS will make sure you do.

When and How Often Do I File?

Taxes are filed once a year for the income you earned during the previous calendar year. In other words, your tax return reports all the money you made from January 1st through December 31st of the previous year.

Do I Even Need to File?

Not everyone *has* to file taxes, but most working adults do. The IRS expects a federal tax return if your income goes past a certain threshold (check irs.gov if you like living dangerously). You also need to file if you're self-employed, got taxes withheld and want your refund back, collected unemployment or other government payments, or earned money in more than one state.

Even if you're technically off the hook, filing can actually put money back in your pocket—imagine that. Here's when you *definitely* need to file:

- You earned more than the standard deduction ($14,600 for single filers, and yes, it changes every year).
- You're self-employed and made over $400 because apparently, the IRS wants its cut too.
- You have a 1099 (freelance, side hustles; they see you).
- You want a refund for taxes you overpaid.
- You got health insurance through the Marketplace.
- You paid college tuition and want education credits (finally, something in your favor).

Even if your earnings are below the threshold, filing can still be worth it if taxes were taken from your paycheck. You might actually get some money back instead of just giving the IRS a freebie.

Understanding Tax Forms

Throughout the year, you'll get hit with a handful of tax forms, each one demanding your attention like an overly clingy ex. First up is the **W-4**, the form you fill out when you start a job. It basically tells your employer how much tax to sneak out of your paycheck—too little, and you'll get a "surprise" bill later; too much, and congrats, you just gave Uncle Sam an interest-free loan. Then comes the **W-2**, your end-of-year report card from your employer, showing exactly how much you earned and how much tax has already been taken. Check it carefully, because you don't want any "creative accounting" on their part messing with your money. If you do freelance work, earn interest, or get dividends, say hello to the **1099 forms**, which tell the IRS,

"Yep, this person made some extra cash." And don't forget the random other forms—like **1098** for mortgage interest or **1095** for health insurance—because apparently even your home and your doctor visits want in on the tax fun. Keep all of these forms organized in a folder or secure digital file. Trust me, when tax season rolls around, you'll thank yourself for not letting Uncle Sam's paperwork turn your life into chaos.

Form	What is it
W-2	Shows how much you made and how much tax your employer withheld
1099-NEC	Reports self-employment or contractor income
1099-K	Reports income from platforms like PayPal, Cash App, Uber, DoorDash
1098-T	Reports college tuition payments (used for education credits)
W-4	You fill this out when you start a job to tell your employer how much tax to withhold
1095-A	Proves you had health insurance through the government Marketplace

Tax Credits vs. Deductions – What's the Difference?

Ah, the classic showdown: tax deductions vs. tax credits, like two friends who sound similar but do totally different things. Deductions are the quiet ones; they lower your taxable income. So if you made $30,000 and managed to claim $2,000 in deductions, the IRS pretends you only earned $28,000 when figuring out your taxes. Not bad, right? Credits, on the other hand, are the overachievers; they cut your actual tax bill, dollar for dollar. Owe $1,000 and qualify for a $1,000 credit? Boom. You owe nothing. It's like having a coupon for Uncle Sam himself. The key takeaway: deductions help reduce the size of the slice the IRS takes, while credits attack the actual bill. Both are great, but credits? That's the one that feels like a win.

Here are some common tax deductions:

- Student loan interest
- Contributions to retirement accounts (like a traditional IRA)
- Charitable donations

Here are some common tax credits:

- Earned Income Tax Credit (EITC) – for low to moderate earners
- American Opportunity Credit – for college tuition (up to $2,500)
- Lifetime Learning Credit – for ongoing education
- Child Tax Credit – for parents

Some credits are refundable, meaning you can still get a refund even if you don't owe anything.

What If You're Self-Employed, a Contractor, or a Freelancer?

If you're a contractor, doing freelance work, running a small business, or working gig jobs like Uber or Instacart, nobody is taking taxes out for you. You'll normally receive a 1099-NEC form, and that means you have to pay your own taxes.

- You may need to file quarterly estimated taxes (every 3 months).
- Keep good records of income and expenses; your laptop, Wi-Fi, gas, and supplies might be deductible.

Set aside 25%–30% of everything you earn to cover taxes. You can use apps like QuickBooks Self-Employed or Wave to track your income and keep receipts.

How Do I File?

You've got options, and it doesn't have to be scary when it comes time to file. There are several apps and software you can use to file your taxes, depending on your situation:

1. Free Tools (if you qualify)

- IRS Free File: Visit www.irs.gov to access a list of partnered companies that offer free tax filing for individuals with income below $73,000. It's an easy way to file your taxes without paying for software or a tax preparer.
- You can use Cash App Taxes and Credit Karma Tax to file your taxes quickly and for free if your situation is relatively straightforward. Both platforms guide you through entering your income, deductions, and credits, then calculate your refund or amount owed. They're designed to be user-friendly, letting you file federal and state returns without paying for software.

2. Tax Software

- TurboTax, H&R Block, TaxAct: Walk you through step-by-step
- Good for W-2 jobs or light gig work
- Costs vary depending on your situation

3. Hire a Tax Preparer or CPA

- Best for complicated situations (like self-employment, home ownership, multiple income sources, or itemizing)
- Usually costs $100–$400+, but may save you time and stress

Tax Filing Season and Deadlines

There are several dates you need to mark on your calendar when it comes to tax season. Missing these can lead to penalties, late fees, or even missing out on your refund.

Date	What It Means
January 31st	Employers must send out W-2s and 1099s
April 15	Deadline to file taxes (or request an extension)
June 15 / Sept 15 / Jan 15	Quarterly tax due dates (for freelancers and gig workers)

W-2 & 1099 Deadline (usually by January 31st): By the end of January, your job (and any side gigs or freelance work) should send you your W-2 or 1099 forms. These show how much money you made and how much was taken out for taxes. Don't file until you've got all of these in hand.

Tax season usually kicks off around mid-January, when the IRS officially starts accepting returns. The earlier you file, the sooner you can get your refund if you're owed one, so don't drag your feet.

Tax Day is typically April 15th. This is the deadline to either file your tax return or request an extension. If you owe the IRS, it's also the day your payment is due; miss it, and interest and penalties start piling up immediately. Sometimes the date is extended, but it's safest to plan as if April 15th is set in stone.

If you can't get everything together in time, you can file for a free extension. But just remember: an extension gives you more time to file, not to pay. The IRS charges interest on any unpaid balance starting the day after Tax Day, usually around 8%–10%, and there can also be a late payment penalty of 0.5% per month, up to 25% of the amount owed.

For example, if you owed $1,000 and didn't pay by April 15, interest starts adding up daily on that $1,000 the next day, and after a month, you'd also owe a $5 penalty—and it keeps growing the longer you wait.

Don't forget state taxes. Some states have different deadlines or require different forms, so check your state's tax website to make sure you're covered and avoid surprises.

What If You Can't Pay Your Taxes?

Not being able to pay the full amount doesn't mean you get to ignore the IRS. Skipping your return only makes things worse because penalties and interest start piling up like an unwelcome surprise party. The silver lining is that the IRS actually offers payment plans, letting you spread what you owe over months and even years, so it doesn't completely ruin your life. You can set one up when you file or apply online at irs.gov. Filing on time, even if your bank account is crying, is always smarter than waiting and watching the penalties snowball.

What Happens If I Don't File?

If you're owed a refund and don't file, congratulations, you have three whole years to file until the government keeps your money. If you owe taxes and ignore paying them, you'll be forced to face penalties, interest, and maybe even wage garnishment, fun right? The IRS always gets what it's owed, so pretending it will go away only digs a deeper hole. Do yourself a favor and deal with it before it turns into a nightmare.

Final Tips to Make Tax Season Easier:

- File early: The earlier you file, the sooner you'll receive your refund.
- Use direct deposit: It's faster and safer than waiting for a paper check.
- Keep everything: Tax forms, receipts, and records. Hold onto them for at least 3 years.
- Double-check your info: Typos in your Social Security number or bank account info can delay your refund.

Final Thought

Taxes aren't fun. Nobody's throwing a party over W-2s and 1099s. But they don't have to be scary either. Once you get the hang of the basics: what to file, what to claim, and when to hit "submit," you've already earned yourself a major adulting gold star.

The key to success as far as taxes go is to stay organized, don't wait until April 14th at 11:59 p.m. (you know who you are), and don't be afraid to ask for help. Google is cool, but sometimes you need a real human who understands the difference between a deduction and a write-off.

Just remember, you got this. And hey, if you can survive a group project in college or Thanksgiving with your loud relatives, you can definitely handle tax season.

6

"You Wanna Know What's More Important Than Throwin' Away Money At The Strip Club? Credit" ~ Jay-Z

Credit Isn't Free Money: Swipe Like You Have Sense

Becoming an adult means learning a lot of things nobody bothered to teach us in school, and credit is one of the most important. In *The Story of O.J.*, Jay-Z makes a simple but powerful point about priorities—short-term spending might feel good in the moment, but it doesn't build anything lasting. Credit does. Flashy purchases come and go, but your credit history sticks around, quietly shaping your options. Good credit opens doors to apartments, cars, lower interest rates, and opportunities, while bad credit makes everything more expensive. That's the lesson many people don't fully understand until they've already learned it the hard way.

Credit isn't free money, and it's definitely not "extra" money.

It's a test of how responsible you are with what you borrow. Your credit history quietly follows you into almost every adult decision—renting an apartment, buying a car, opening utilities, getting a credit card, and sometimes even landing a job. When your credit is solid, things move smoothly. When it's bad or nonexistent, you pay more, wait longer, or get told no altogether. This chapter is about learning how to use credit wisely, so it works for you instead of against you.

What Is Credit Really? That Magical Number That Judges You Silently

Credit is essentially borrowed money you're promising to pay back, usually with interest, within a certain amount of time. It's like when a friend spots you $20 for gas and you say you'll get it back on payday. Only in the adult world, your lender is a bank or credit card company, and they're definitely keeping receipts.

When you borrow money, a record of your behavior is created: your payment history, how much you owe, how long you've been borrowing, and what types of credit you use. This information becomes your credit report, and it's used to calculate your credit score, a three-digit number that represents your financial reputation, which ranges from 300 - 850. The higher your credit score, the better.

Care Now or Cry Later: Your Credit's Watching

Think of your credit score like your adulting GPA; the higher it is, the more doors open and the fewer headaches you deal with. Credit scores usually run from about 300 to 850, and here's the lowdown: if you're hanging out on the low end, let's just say your financial "report card" is screaming for summer school. Here's the lowdown on credit scores:

- **300−579: Poor** − Basically, you're that kid nobody wants to sit next to. High interest rates, landlords giving you side-eye, lenders saying "nope."
- **580−669: Fair** − Not a disaster, but expect some annoyed lenders and higher interest rates.
- **670−739: Good** − You're solid. Most doors open, rates are decent, and people don't cringe when they see your score.
- **740−799: Very Good** − Congrats, you're adulting well. Lenders love you, rates are sweet, and approval is usually easy.
- **800−850: Excellent** − The VIP lounge of credit. You get the best rates, and lenders are practically rolling out a red carpet.

Why does it matter if you have good credit or not? Because your credit touches nearly every corner of your adult life. Landlords check it when you're trying to rent an apartment, just to make sure you actually pay bills on time. If you're buying a car or a home, your score determines not only whether you get approved but also how much interest you'll be stuck paying. Some employers—especially in finance—look at your credit report, figuring if you can handle your own money, you might be trusted to handle theirs. Even everyday essentials like utilities or phone plans can hit a snag, since bad credit often means you'll have to cough up a hefty deposit before you can even flip a switch or send a text.

Hold on to your credit like it's the platinum key to life.

Never co-sign or lend it to someone else. I know, I know—they'll swear up and down that they'll pay the car note or rent on time. But let's be real—if they were truly responsible with money, they wouldn't need your signature in the first place. The bank already looked at them and said, "Absolutely not," so why would you jump in as the backup plan? Co-signing is basically handing your car keys to someone who just failed their driving test—you *know* they're going to crash, but now it's your insurance going up. When they miss a payment, your credit takes the hit, collections start blowing up your phone, and suddenly you're cleaning up a financial mess you didn't even create. And don't think family or best friends get a free pass—money drama ruins relationships faster than cheating. Bottom line: protect your credit like it's your social security number, because once it's trashed, the cleanup is a long, expensive, stressful process.

Credit 101: The Basics

Let's break down the different types of credit you're likely to encounter so you know what you're dealing with and how to handle it like a responsible adult.

- **Credit Cards:** Basically a "revolving door of debt." You swipe, you pay it back (hopefully), and then you swipe again. Sounds fun until you realize interest is charged daily, which means every time you procrastinate paying it off, the bank is out here collecting coins like Mario. Moral of the story? Pay early unless you enjoy donating free money to billion-dollar banks.

- **Loans:** Student, personal, auto, business—pick your poison. A loan is just a fancy way of saying, "Here's some money, but you'll owe us for the rest of your natural life." Depending on the type of loan, you'll be paying it back anywhere from a few months to, oh, I don't know, until your grandkids graduate. And miss a payment? Congratulations, you just made your credit score cry.
- **Lines of Credit:** Think of it as the bougie cousin of credit cards. Same idea—borrow, pay back, borrow again—but usually for bigger expenses, like fixing your house or saving your business from drowning. Flexible? Yes. Dangerous if you don't manage it? Also yes.

Every time you borrow and repay, you're building your credit story. Pay on time, or better yet, early—every month, because the sooner you pay, the less interest piles up and the more your score climbs. Treat your credit like your adult report card. If you ignore it, you're setting yourself up for some painful lessons.

Credit: The Only Thing You Want to Grow Fast (Besides Your Bank Account)

I know building credit when you don't have any feels a lot like trying to get a job that wants you to have experience, but you're fresh out of college. How Sway? It's frustrating but not impossible. The key is to start small. One of the easiest ways to build credit is by opening a secured credit card. With a secured card, you put down a deposit, let's say $500, and that becomes your credit limit. You can use it for everyday things like gas or groceries, but the trick is to pay it off in full every month. Another smart move to build credit is becoming an authorized user on someone else's credit card, like a parent or trusted family member who has good credit and pays their bills on time. I did this for my daughter, and by the time she was 21, she already had a 700 credit score. It works. The biggest thing to remember is that credit is all about consistency. Pay on time, keep your balances low, and give it time. Credit isn't built overnight; it's a marathon, not a sprint.

Here's a list of popular credit card companies that offer secured credit cards, especially good for people who are just starting to build credit:

Discover – *Discover it® Secured Credit Card*

- No annual fee
- Cash back rewards (rare for secured cards)
- Automatically reviews your account for an upgrade to an unsecured card

Capital One – *Capital One Platinum Secured Credit Card*

- Low minimum deposit starting at $49, $99, or $200 (depending on creditworthiness)
- No annual fee
- Opportunity for a credit line increase with on-time payments

Chime – *Chime Credit Builder Secured Visa® Credit Card*

- No credit check to apply

- No annual fee or interest
- Requires a Chime Checking Account

Citi – *Citi® Secured Mastercard®*

- No annual fee
- Helps build credit with responsible use
- Requires a security deposit equal to your credit limit

Bank of America – *BankAmericard® Secured Credit Card*

- $200 minimum security deposit
- No annual fee
- Possible graduation to unsecured after responsible use

OpenSky® – *OpenSky® Secured Visa® Credit Card*

- No credit check to apply
- $35 annual fee
- Reports to all three major credit bureaus

U.S. Bank – *U.S. Bank Secured Visa® Card*

- $300 minimum deposit
- Annual fee: $29
- Reports to all three major credit bureaus

Meet the Credit Bureaus: Because One Company Judging You Just Wasn't Enough

I bet you didn't know there are *three* credit bureaus out here in these financial streets keeping tabs on your every financial move like a nosy neighbor with a clipboard. Yep, three. And they're not just chillin', they're standing between you and that cute new apartment, your dream car, or that shiny new credit card you've been eyeing. Meet the Big Three: Experian, Equifax, and TransUnion. Basically, the Destiny's Child of credit reporting, but no one can agree on who's Beyoncé.

These credit bureaus collect all the tea from your lenders and put it into a little report that says, "This is how responsible (or not) you are with money." They keep tabs on who you borrowed from, how much you still owe, what your monthly payments look like, your due dates, and whether you pay on time or if you're out here ghosting your bills like a bad Tinder date.

Now here's the kicker: each bureau might have *slightly* different info. Why, you ask? Because not every lender reports to all three, and each one has its own special way of scoring you, like they're out here playing financial American Idol. One uses FICO, the other might use VantageScore, and you? You're just hoping somebody gives you a passing grade.

Both FICO (that's short for Fair Isaac Corporation, not your cousin's nickname) and VantageScore use different formulas, but they look at the same basics: payment history, credit usage, how long you've had credit, types of credit, and new credit. But lenders tend to trust FICO a little more, so if you're trying to get approved, that's the score you want to keep. Each bureau might have slightly different data because not all creditors report to all three. That's why your score can vary depending on where it's pulled from.

Here's the breakdown of factors that are considered to formulate your credit score on the report:

- Payment History (35%) – Pay on time. Every time.
- Amounts Owed (30%) – Don't max out your cards. Keep your usage below 30%.
- Length of Credit History (15%) – The longer your accounts stay open (and in good standing), the better.
- Credit Mix (10%) – A variety of accounts (loans, credit cards, etc.) shows you can handle different types of credit.
- New Credit (10%) – Opening too many accounts at once can hurt you.

Monitor Your Credit Like Your Ex Is Monitoring You

One thing you definitely need to do is stay on top of your credit. I monitor all three of my credit reports on a monthly basis. What you don't want is a negative mark to hit your credit. It takes months, even years, to build up your credit, but it takes one missed payment to bring it down instantly. So, use everything you can to maintain it. You're entitled to one free credit report from each bureau every year from AnnualCreditReport.com. Use it! Check for errors, identity theft, or accounts you don't recognize. Dispute anything that looks off. Equifax was involved in a major data breach in 2017, so keep an eye on your info. Each credit bureau has its own site where you can check your credit, but other sites like NerdWallet, Credit Karma, and WalletHub let you compare all three bureaus in one place.

Each site offers different tools to help you stay on top of things:

- Experian - Known for Experian Boost, which lets you add on-time utility, phone, and even streaming service payments to your credit report. It can give your score a little boost, especially if you're just starting out or rebuilding.
- TransUnion - Offers tools like CreditView Dashboard (often through your bank or credit card) and TrueIdentity, a free identity protection service that includes credit monitoring and the ability to lock/unlock your TransUnion report.
- Equifax offers Equifax Core Credit, a free tool that provides access to your monthly Equifax credit report and VantageScore. For more robust features, their paid Equifax Credit Monitor tracks changes to your credit, sends alerts, and helps you spot potential fraud. With Credit Lock, you can quickly lock or unlock your Equifax report to prevent unauthorized access. Their premium Equifax Complete service combines credit monitoring and identity theft protection with up to $1 million in ID theft insurance, offering comprehensive protection and peace of mind.

Tips to Build and Maintain Good Credit

- Pay your bills on time – Set reminders or use auto-pay to stay on track.
- Keep your balances low – Ideally under 30% of your credit limit.
- Check your credit reports regularly – Mistakes happen, and you can dispute errors.
- Don't close old accounts unnecessarily – Especially your

oldest ones.

- Only apply for new credit when necessary – Too many inquiries can ding your score.

Things That Tank Your Credit Faster Than a Text from Your Ex

Let's be real, life happens, and sometimes bills don't get paid on time. But knowing what can mess up your credit is half the battle. Here's what you might see pop up on your credit report if things go sideways:

- Late Payments: If you're more than 30 days late on a credit card loan or car payment, that late payment is getting reported. And the later it is, like 60 or 90 days, the worse it looks. Even one missed payment can drag your score down.
- Collections: If you ignore a bill long enough (unpaid medical bills or phone bills), it can get sent to collections. Once that happens, the collection agency reports it, and your credit score takes a hit.
- Charge-Offs: A charge-off happens when a creditor basically says, "We're done trying to get this money." It doesn't mean the debt disappears; you still owe it, but now it's sitting on your report like a big red flag.
- Repossessions: When you miss enough car payments, the lender can come and get that car. And yep, the repo gets slapped on your credit report, making it harder to get approved for loans in the future.
- Defaulted Student Loans: Student loans don't play. If you ignore your payments for too long, they go into default, and that can stick to your credit report like glue, making it hard to borrow for anything else.

- Too Many Hard Inquiries: Every time you apply for a credit card or loan, a hard inquiry gets added to your report. One or two? No big deal. But applying for 5-6 cards in a month? Even though they'll say it's not going to affect your report, they're lying. That's a red flag to lenders.

Collections, charge-offs, late payments, and repossessions don't just vanish into thin air—they can haunt your credit report for up to seven long years. That means every financial mistake you make today could still be following you around years from now, messing with your ability to get approved for things you want. Think about it: seven years is enough time to graduate high school, finish college, or binge-watch every show on Netflix twice. And unlike some exes, these marks don't just block you on social media and disappear—they hang on and pop up every time someone checks your credit. The bottom line? Pay attention to what you're doing with your money, because those choices leave receipts, and the credit bureaus keep them filed for almost a decade.

Moral of the story? Stay on top of your payments, monitor your credit regularly, and if you fall behind, don't ghost your bills. Handle it before it snowballs into a bigger problem. Most credit card and loan companies are *actually* willing to help if you just pick up the phone and explain what's going on. Some options they might offer include:

- Payment deferral: Pushing back your due date to give you breathing room.
- Account forbearance or temporary hold: Pressing pause on payments without penalties while you get back on your feet.

- Hardship programs: Some credit cards offer these quietly; you'll need to ask. If you're temporarily unemployed and can show proof, they may cover your minimum monthly payment, waive late fees, temporarily reduce your interest rate, or pause your account activity without it wrecking your credit.

Bottom line: Communication is free. Ignoring bills is expensive. All of these can seriously impact your credit, but they're not a life sentence. Just like I did, you can rebuild. It takes time, patience, and consistency, but it's worth it.

The Glow-Up Your Credit Deserves

Whether you're building credit for the first time or trying to recover after a setback like missed payments, collections, or even bankruptcy, you can bounce back. It won't be overnight, but with the right moves, you can rebuild your credit and boost your score over time. Consistency and patience are the keys. Getting a secured credit card can be a start to making on-time payments and keeping your credit utilization low. There are several ways to rebuild your credit and prove to lenders you're serious about managing money the right way.

My Story: That Time My Credit Took a Detour

I'm going to be totally transparent with you. There was a time in my life when I thought I had it all under control. I was paying my bills using my credit cards responsibly, doing all the "adult" things. Then life happened. I lost my job unexpectedly. At first, I tried to keep up robbing Peter to pay Paul, using one credit card to pay another and bouncing checks just to keep the lights on.

But eventually, the bills piled up, the phone calls from collectors wouldn't stop, and I just couldn't keep up because the check from unemployment didn't cover my lifestyle, and I had run through the little savings I had. I had to make one of the hardest decisions of my life: filing for Chapter 7 bankruptcy. I was ashamed, and I felt like I had failed at life.

But here's what I learned: bankruptcy isn't the end. It's a restart. It gave me a chance to breathe, reset, and rebuild. And I did rebuild. It took time, discipline, and a whole lot of financial education. But it's possible. So don't let one chapter of your life define the whole story.

Life Happens: Navigating Setbacks

Even if you're doing everything "right," paying your bills on time, budgeting, and making smart money decisions, life has a funny way of throwing curveballs. Getting laid off from your job can throw your whole budget out of whack. A family crisis might force you to dip into your savings or take on unexpected debt.

These moments can wreck your finances faster than you ever expected. That's why having good credit, savings, and an emergency fund matters; it gives you a safety net when life happens. And if you don't have those yet, don't stress. You can always start now.

If you're struggling to keep up:

- Contact your creditors before you miss payments; they may

be willing to work with you.
- Look into credit counseling or nonprofit debt management programs.
- Know your rights. The Fair Credit Reporting Act protects you from misinformation on your credit reports.
- And if it comes to bankruptcy, understand that it's not the end. It's a new beginning.

Final Thought

Use credit as a tool, not a crutch. Credit is powerful, baby. Like, Beyoncé-in-a-power-suit powerful. But if you don't respect it, it *will* humble you faster than an overdraft alert on payday. The key is to use it *wisely*. Translation: don't go swiping like you're on a game show. Keep your spending cute and your balance low.

Learn from your mistakes, and definitely mine. I took the scenic route through Credit Struggle Land so *you* don't have to. And please don't let one financial flop have you out here thinking your money story is over; it's not. You've got what it takes to build something solid.

This chapter handed you the blueprint. Now it's your move. Just remember: credit is a tool, not a free-for-all shopping pass. Build smart, stay ready, and make that credit work *for* you, not the other way around.

7

"Wood Floors In The New Apartment, Couture From the Stores Department" ~ Kanye West

Apartment 101: Keys, Leases, and Rent Receipts

In the song *Flashing Lights*, Kanye West paints a picture of finally upgrading your lifestyle—moving into a nicer apartment, enjoying independence, and feeling like you've officially made it. And sure, wood floors, good lighting, and a place that feels grown is a flex. But what that line really represents is the moment people chase without fully understanding the responsibility that comes with it. Because apartment living isn't just about aesthetics; it's about lease terms, security deposits, rent that's due whether you love the place or not, and real consequences if you fall behind. Ignore the fine print, and that dream apartment can quickly turn into a financial headache, a drained bank account, or an eviction notice taped to the door. This chapter is here to help you enjoy the upgrade—without letting it upgrade your stress.

Where Do You Even Start to Look?

Apartment hunting can feel like a full-time job, except nobody's giving you a paycheck for it. Luckily, there are a ton of websites and apps designed to make your life easier because, apparently, even finding a place to live now requires a search engine degree.

There are tons of apartment websites and apps out there that make it easier to scroll through listings, compare prices, and find a spot that actually fits your budget and lifestyle. Here are some to kick off your quest:

- Zillow Rentals: Filters for days, neighborhood tea, and alerts for price drops.
- Apartments.com: Virtual tours so you can stalk your future crib without leaving your couch.
- Hot Pads: Good for finding those "hidden gems" (aka places no one else wants).
- Craigslist: Still alive, but scam central, buyer beware.
- Facebook Marketplace/Groups: Because apparently, everyone's now a landlord or subletter. Also, scams lurk here, too, so be careful and investigate thoroughly when using this platform.

Before you click "apply," you gotta know two things: your budget and what you absolutely *can't* live without. Spoiler: "luxury rooftop pool" usually isn't on the list.

Know Your Budget (Because Your Bank Account Doesn't Lie)

Here's the golden rule: keep your rent at 30% or less of your monthly income. So, if you pull in $3,000 a month, aim for about $1,000 in rent. Yeah, I know. Good luck finding that in most cities without sharing a broom closet with a cat. But don't get cute trying to impress Instagram with your "luxury" digs you can't actually afford. I know it's hard when you see Instagram influencers living in high rises with floor-to-ceiling windows in new luxury buildings, but your time will come to live that high life too. But for now, stay within a tight budget. Besides, as long as you decorate your apartment nicely, no one knows where you live or what it looks like on the outside.

And rent isn't the only money pit. You'll also have to fork over cash for:

- Utilities (electricity, gas, water, trash, yes, trash costs money now)
- Internet (because Wi-Fi is survival, not a luxury)
- Renters insurance (not just for the paranoid, trust me)
- Parking fees (if you have a car and don't want it to get towed)
- Pet fees (because Fluffy isn't free)

Be honest with yourself, just because you *qualify* for a fancy apartment doesn't mean you should sign on the dotted line. Learn from my mistakes: living paycheck to paycheck is not the move

Understanding the Lease (Read It or Regret It)

Your lease isn't just some casual piece of paper you sign so you can get the keys and start moving your couch in—it's a legally binding contract. Think of it like a sneaky little trap, written in legal jargon that looks harmless at first glance but can cost you big if you don't pay attention. That's why you have to read the whole thing. Yep, every single boring line, even the ones that make your eyes glaze over. The fine print is where landlords hide all the "gotchas," like rules about breaking your lease, sneaky fees, or whether you can hang that 65-inch TV without losing your security deposit. Some leases even throw in wild restrictions like no overnight guests for more than a few days, or you're responsible for all repairs over $50, even if the sink explodes. Bottom line: don't skim. Read, highlight, and if you don't understand something, ask. Because once your signature is on that paper, saying "I didn't know" won't save you.

Here's the lowdown on lease contracts:

- Lease Terms: Usually 12 months, but sometimes can be shorter, 3-6 months, or longer up to 24 months. Month-to-month leases are available and more flexible, but usually more expensive.
- Security Deposit: Deposits are usually 1–2 months' rent, which is refundable if you don't trash the place. Some places give move-in specials, but they'll check your credit first, so make sure your credit is on point.
- Utilities Included: Some leases include these; others leave you holding the bill. Don't assume water or heat is free.
- Rent Due Date: Usually the 1st of the month with a grace

period until the 5th (if you're lucky). Pay late, and fees come knocking, and sometimes your credit gets bruised.

- Late Rent: Miss a rent payment, and you get late fees plus the looming threat of eviction. Eviction? Yeah, that's landlord code for "you're officially blacklisted in the rental world."

Avoiding Eviction and Staying Ahead (No One Wants That Drama)

If you're going to be late on rent, the worst thing you can do is ghost your landlord. Pick up the phone and call them as soon as you know you'll be short. Being upfront shows that you're responsible, even if your bank account might say otherwise, and it can buy you some much-needed grace time. Sometimes that honesty gets you a few extra days before late penalties kick in, a payment plan to make the number less terrifying, waived or reduced late fees (especially if it's your first time), or even a referral to rental assistance programs. But if you dodge their calls and pretend the problem doesn't exist, eviction proceedings will come at you faster than your Wi-Fi cuts out during a Zoom meeting.

My Story: The Rent Was Due, But the Job Was Gone

When I first got my own place, I *really* thought I had this adulting thing on lock. I had a job, a kid, and a plan. I was out here feeling grown grown. Then, life being the petty queen she is, said: "Hold my beer."

I lost my job. And surprise, surprise, no job means no rent money. I didn't have savings, didn't have a Plan B, just straight-up panic and prayers. And instead of doing the smart, responsible thing, like I don't know, talking to someone in the rental office, I went radio silent.

Looking back, I handled it all the wrong way. But fear, pride, and straight-up embarrassment had me stuck. I didn't want to admit I was struggling. I didn't want to look weak. So I just ghosted my landlord. No calls, no emails, just fear and anxiety.

Guess what that got me? An eviction notice slapped dead on my door like a scarlet letter. That thing hit me like a ton of bricks.

Thankfully, I managed to find a cheaper apartment at the last minute, and I moved out before an eviction hit my record. Talk about a close call. It was humbling, but it saved me from being labeled "the evicted girl" that no landlord wants to deal with.

Real Talk: Why Silence Is the Rent Killer

Ignoring your landlord costs way more than just the rent, I learned that the hard way. When money is tight, it's tempting to avoid the uncomfortable conversation and just hope things somehow work themselves out. But here's the truth: staying silent only makes things worse, and faster than you think. Late fees start piling up, your landlord starts losing patience, and before you know it, you're staring down eviction notices and court dates. Fear and pride won't pay your bills; I know because I tried. And all I got was more stress, a damaged rental history, and an even bigger financial mess to clean up.

What to Say to Your Landlord When You Mess Up:

When reaching out to your landlord, try this grown-up, respect-ful approach that takes responsibility for the mistake, explains what happened, and offers a clear plan to fix it, without making excuses.

> *"Hello [Landlord's Name] I'm dealing with some unex-pected money issues this month. I might need a few extra days to pay rent. I'm serious about staying on good terms and wanted to check if we could work something out."*

Being honest and proactive might not erase your rent, but it could buy you time and protect your rental history.

Final Lesson: Just because you can pay your rent today doesn't mean you'll be able to tomorrow. Budget for emergencies or be ready to pack up quickly because, honey, if eviction day rolls around, they will toss your personal belongings on the curb like yesterday's trash. Believe that.

Keep Rent Stress Low (Yes, It's Possible)

Paying rent can be one of the biggest stressors of adulting, especially when you're juggling bills, student loans, and other monthly expenses. Keeping that stress in check comes down to planning and a little discipline. One smart move is to align your rent with your paychecks by breaking it into smaller chunks, so you're not panicking every first of the month. Another lifesaver is building a dedicated "rent fund" with at least six months' worth of rent tucked away for emergencies—a safety net that gives you some breathing room. And if your paycheck barely stretches far enough, consider picking up a side hustle. Whether it's a part-time job or gig work like DoorDash, Uber, or Lyft, that extra income can make the difference between stressing over rent and actually breathing easy.

Thankfully, technology has your back. Apps like **Deferit.com**, **GetFlex.com**, and **MyZenBase.com** let you split your rent into smaller, more manageable payments each month. Some even allow you to delay or schedule payments automatically, spreading your rent across multiple paychecks or giving you extra wiggle room in tight months. Are you living with roommates? These apps handle that too. Everyone can pay their share directly through the platform, no awkward IOUs, no chasing anyone down on text, or I'll CashApp you later. You can track payments, see upcoming due dates, and get reminders, so late fees don't sneak up on you.

Using rent-splitting apps isn't about avoiding responsibility; it's about managing your money smarter. When your rent is organized and predictable, you're free to focus on building savings, paying down debt, or stacking funds for your next big move. Less stress, more control, and maybe even room for a latte or two.

Roommates: The Rent Hack That Can Save Your Wallet (or Wreck Your Sanity)

Not every city is affordable; some of these rents are downright disrespectful. But there are always ways to make it work, and one of the smartest moves early on is getting a roommate. Sharing rent, utilities, and even household expenses like internet and toilet paper can seriously cut your monthly costs. That's more money for savings, debt payments, or you know...actually enjoying your life.

Splitting rent can literally save your life (and your wallet). It can also give you access to a better neighborhood, a nicer apartment, or just a little breathing room financially. But before you go adding "Roomie Needed" to your IG story, choose wisely.

Because while a roommate can be a blessing, the *wrong* roommate can turn your dream apartment into a full-blown horror movie. And I'm not being dramatic, have you seen the movie *Single White Female*? If not, do yourself a favor and watch it before you commit to splitting your living space with somebody who might just rearrange your life (and not in a good way).

Bottom line, roommates can be clutch, but don't just move in with anyone who breathes. Interview them like you're casting for a reality show because trust me, living with someone is a big deal.

Here are some things you need to know before giving your new roommate the final rose:

- Do they have a criminal record?
- Do they have a steady income?
- Do they have good credit, and what's their credit score?
- Can they keep their socks off the floor? How clean are they?
- Will they pay bills on time or ghost you?
- Have they ever been evicted or broken a lease?

These are all important questions that need to be asked ahead of time. Also, make sure to draft a roommate agreement. Even the best friendships get ugly over who's buying toilet paper. Writing out who pays what, how you'll handle groceries or guests, and what happens if someone wants to move out can save your friendship and your finances.

Affordable Housing: Yes, It Exists (And No, You Don't Have to Live in a Shack)

If your budget's tighter than your jeans after Thanksgiving dinner, don't automatically assume you're doomed to live in some sketchy basement with a leaky ceiling and roommates who steal your food. Believe it or not, there *are* housing options out there designed to help folks with lower or moderate incomes live safely and affordably. You just gotta know where (and how) to look. Because they're not exactly handing out flyers on the street corner.

It's called income-based housing, also known as subsidized or affordable housing. Basically, your rent is based on how much you earn. Wild concept, right? Instead of coughing up half your check just to have a roof over your head, you typically only pay about 30% of your monthly income in rent. The rest is covered by government programs, non-profits, or private landlords who team up with HUD (aka the U.S. Department of Housing and Urban Development). There *is* help out there, you just have to be willing to do a little digging, and maybe wait on a list longer than the Chick-fil-A drive-thru on a Sunday... oh wait.

Types of income-based housing:

- *Low-Income Housing Tax Credit (LIHTC):* Landlords get tax breaks for offering reduced rent. These places look like regular apartments; you just pay less. You'll need to qualify based on income and credit, but it's a solid option if you can find one.

- *Hidden Gems:* Affordable Units in Luxury Apartments. Yep, even those fancy buildings with rooftop pools and dog spas are often *required by law* to offer a small percentage of income-based units. But they won't be plastering that on billboards. You have to ask. Walk your confident self into that leasing office and say, *"Do y'all offer any affordable units or income-based apartments?"* You might be surprised. Don't ever be ashamed to get what's available for you.

- *Section 8 (Housing Choice Vouchers):* The government helps pay your rent in *regular* apartments (if the landlord accepts vouchers). You pay 30–40% of your income, and the government covers the rest. The waitlist is longer than a CVS receipt, but it's worth the hustle.

- Public Housing: Run by your local housing authority. You live in government-owned buildings and pay about 30% of your income. Not fancy, but solid and stable (depending on the location).

What is Rent Control?

Rent-controlled or rent-stabilized housing works a little differently from regular rentals. These are privately owned apartments where laws cap how much rent can go up each year, making it easier to predict and manage your long-term housing costs. Not every city offers rent control, but places like New York City, San Francisco, Washington D.C., Los Angeles, Oakland, and Berkeley are known for it. If you're moving somewhere with rent control, look for clues in listings that mention "rent-stabilized" or "under rent control," landlords who've been part of these programs for years, or older buildings, which are often covered by rent regulations. Keep in mind, some properties come with income requirements or specific lease rules, so always ask questions and read the lease carefully before signing.

How to Find These Units

- Use websites like AffordableHousing.com or your local housing authority's site to search for income-based rentals.
- Call property management companies and ask if they offer LIHTC units or participate in Section 8.
- Set up alerts on rental sites like Zillow or Apartments.com with filters for "income-restricted" or "affordable" housing.
- Connect with local nonprofits that specialize in housing services, and they can help you navigate the system.

Negotiate: If a place has been listed for a while, landlords may be open to lowering the rent or offering perks (such as free parking or reduced move-in fees).

And don't be afraid to walk away. If something feels off, whether it's the landlord, the lease, or the apartment itself, trust your gut.

Before You Sign Your Name on the Dotted Line

1. Do a Walkthrough Before Signing the Lease. Check for damages, test appliances, turn on faucets and flush toilets, and document everything with photos or video. Don't skip this step; your security deposit depends on it.

2. Read Every Word of the Lease - Yes, it's long and boring, but it's legally binding. Know what happens if you break the lease early, what fees apply, and what rules you're agreeing to.

3. Always Check What's Included - Is water included? Is electric or gas included? Wi-Fi? Don't just assume. Ask what's covered and what you'll need to pay separately.

4. Avoid Scams - Never send money or pay a deposit before seeing the place in person or through a verified virtual tour, before signing a lease. Especially if you're renting from a private owner. If it sounds too good to be true, it probably is.

5. Budget for Moving Costs - Don't just think about the rent; factor in the cost of a moving truck, boxes, taking time off work, and maybe even hiring movers. Yeah, movers can be expensive, but they're a whole lot more dependable than that flaky friend who swears they'll help you "as long as nothing comes up." Pro tip: haul the smaller boxes yourself and pay the movers to deal with the big, heavy items like the sofa or dresser. That way, you cut down on their time, because when it comes to moving, the clock is ticking, and every tick is costing you money.

6. Set a Calendar Reminder for Rent - Even if you've automated it, set a reminder. Some landlords still charge fees even if it's just one day late.

7. Avoid Rent Shock - If your lease is ending soon, ask about renewal terms early. Many landlords raise rent at renewal time, and you'll want time to decide if you'll stay or move.

8. Location vs. Looks - That shiny apartment won't mean much if it's far from work, school, or public transportation. Consider commute, safety, and nearby amenities.

9. Don't Max Out Your Budget - Just because you qualify for $2,000/month doesn't mean you should spend that much. Give yourself breathing room for the unexpected.

Don't Forget the Upfront Costs. Besides the first month's rent, you'll likely need:

- Security deposit (1–2 months' rent)
- Application fee
- Admin fee or move-in fee
- Amenities fee
- Utility setup deposit

Final Thought

Your first apartment should feel like a win, not a financial trap. Don't get played by shiny granite countertops, wood floors, and rooftop pools if it means you're one missed paycheck away from back on the couch at your momma's house. Budget smart, read your lease thoroughly, and always keep a backup plan. And hey, if you mess up, you're not alone. We all stumble. Just don't stay down.

8

"I Was Gamblin' With My Life, For Sure, I Was Livin' Like I Had Life Insurance" ~ Tee Grizzley

"In Case Sh*t Happens": The Insurance You'll Be Glad You Had

In the song *Life Insurance*, Tee Grizzley raps about moving through life as if nothing bad could happen, taking risks without really thinking about the consequences. That mindset is common when you're young, you feel untouchable, focused on getting ahead, and insurance feels like something you can worry about later. But adulthood has a way of correcting that thinking quickly. One unexpected moment can change everything. Insurance isn't just another bill to pay; it's the protection you wish you had in place when life reminds you that accidents, emergencies, and setbacks don't wait until you feel ready.

When you're starting out, it's easy to overlook insurance

while juggling rent, groceries, and trying to keep your bank account out of the negative. But the truth is, not having the right coverage can turn a bad day into long-term financial damage. A car accident without enough insurance, an unexpected hospital visit, or even a break-in at your apartment can leave you paying thousands out of pocket. These aren't "what if" situations—they happen every day. And without insurance, you're basically betting that nothing will ever go wrong.

This chapter breaks down the types of insurance every adult should understand: health, auto, renters, and life insurance, what they actually cover, how to choose the right amount, and why they matter more than people like to admit. Think of insurance as grown-folk protection: you hope you never need it, but when you do, you'll be glad you didn't gamble with your future.

Because GoFundMe Isn't a Plan: Why You Need Life Insurance Now

When you're young and healthy, life insurance might seem unnecessary. You might think, "I have my whole life ahead of me, I don't need to worry about that yet." But securing life insurance in your twenties can actually be one of the smartest financial decisions you can make for your future. Here's why:

- Cheaper While You're Young – Insurance companies love young, healthy people because you're low-risk. Lock it in now and save yourself thousands later.
- Health Now, Savings Later – Your 20-something body is in its prime. Buy now, and even if life throws you a health curveball later, your rate stays low.

- Cash Value Glow-Up – Permanent life insurance builds cash value you can borrow from later. The earlier you start, the fatter that little money stash can get.
- Day-One Protection – No spouse? No kids? Cool. But life insurance can still cover your funeral costs, debts, and help your family if something happens.
- Perks While You're Young – Riders (a.k.a. policy add-ons) like disability or critical illness coverage are easier and cheaper to get now than later.
- Future-Proof Your Coverage – Lock in a fixed rate before you take on big life stuff—house, kids, business—so you're set without your premiums going up.
- Compound Growth is Your Bestie – Permanent policies grow over time, and starting early means your cash value gets more years to snowball into something big.
- Sleep Easy – Life is unpredictable. Knowing you're covered at the best rate possible, that's financial peace of mind.

Life Insurance: Because Apparently 'Cross Your Fingers and Hope' Isn't a Plan

When it comes to life insurance, there's more than one flavor to choose from, and knowing the difference can save you some serious headaches (and money). The two main types are term life and whole life insurance, but Universal, Burial, and Variable are other types of insurance you also need to know about.

Types of life insurance	Coverage length	Builds cash value?	Death benefit
Term	Temporary — typically 10, 20 or 30 years.	No.	Fixed.
Whole	Lifetime.	Yes.	Fixed.
Universal	Lifetime.	Yes.	Flexible.
Variable	Lifetime.	Yes.	Flexible.
Burial	Lifetime.	Yes.	Fixed.

Term Life Insurance: The Netflix Subscription of Death Planning

Term life is the no-frills, basic cable version of life insurance. It's cheap, simple, and comes with an expiration date—just like that yogurt in the back of your fridge. You pick a life term (10, 20, or 30 years), and if you pass during that time, your loved ones get a nice lump sum payout. If you survive (congrats on not dying), you get... absolutely nothing. Zilch. Just the warm satisfaction of still being alive and the faint sting of knowing all those premiums went down the drain.

This type of insurance is clutch if you just need coverage while you've got major responsibilities—like raising kids, paying off a mortgage, or pretending you understand your 401(k). It's not an investment, there's no savings account hiding inside, and it doesn't come with fancy extras. But because it's bare-bones, it's also way cheaper than other types. Think of it as the ramen noodles of life insurance: not glamorous, but it gets the job done.

Whole Life Insurance: The Clingy Roommate of Insurance

Whole life is like that friend who moves in "just for a few months" and never leaves. Once you sign up, it sticks with you until you die—no expiration date. Premiums are higher than term, but that's because it comes with extra features, like a savings component (a.k.a. "cash value") that grows over time. Sounds fancy, right? But remember, that cash value is basically your money being held hostage by the insurance company until they decide you've earned the privilege of borrowing it back... with interest.

So yes, it's pricier, but it's also reliable. If term life is ramen noodles, whole life is that overpriced meal-prep subscription you convince yourself is an "investment" in your future.

The perk of Whole Life Insurance is that the younger and healthier you are, the cheaper your premium will be. But as you get older—and start collecting bad knees, mystery back pain, and a medicine cabinet full of prescriptions—your premium climbs right along with your risk of passing, so get it as early as possible.

Universal Life Insurance: The 'Choose Your Own Adventure' Policy

Universal life is for people who want "flexibility," which is a nice way of saying you'll constantly be tinkering with it and stressing about whether you funded it enough. You can adjust your premiums and death benefit along the way, which sounds empowering until you realize you basically need to be a part-time accountant to manage it.

The good news? It also builds cash value, which means you

94

can borrow against it later (translation: you're taking a loan from yourself... and yes, charging yourself interest). It's like having a life insurance policy and a moody savings account rolled into one. Great if you like options; not so great if you like simplicity.

Variable Life Insurance – Variable life insurance is a permanent policy that also has a cash value component, but unlike whole or universal life, the cash value is invested in stocks, bonds, or mutual funds. This means the cash value, and sometimes even the death benefit, can go up or down depending on market performance. Because of this investment feature, variable life offers the potential for higher returns, but it also comes with greater risk. It's typically for people who are comfortable with investing and want their life insurance to have growth potential beyond a fixed interest rate.

Burial (Final Expense) Insurance – Burial insurance, also known as final expense insurance, is a small whole life insurance policy specifically meant to cover end-of-life expenses like funeral costs, burial, or medical bills. Coverage amounts are usually lower, ranging from $5,000 to $25,000. It's easier to qualify for, even if you have health issues. While it's technically a form of whole life insurance, it's marketed specifically for those who want to make sure their family isn't financially burdened by funeral costs.

Why It Pays to Start Now

Getting life insurance in your twenties isn't just about "what ifs," it's a smart move for your future. You'll lock in lower premiums, start building cash value early, and protect yourself while you're young and healthy. Whether you're flying solo or building a family, it's one less thing to stress about down the line. Don't wait until it's more expensive or harder to qualify. Start now, you'll thank yourself later.

Health Insurance: Because Google Can't Actually Cure You

Health Insurance is usually the first type of insurance most young adults hear about. It's not just for when you're sick; it helps cover preventive care, routine checkups, and major medical events. Without it, a hospital visit or surgery can quickly lead to unmanageable debt. Health insurance isn't just about keeping you healthy; it's about protecting your finances from unexpected medical expenses.

If your employer offers health insurance, that's usually the most affordable and convenient option. But if they don't or if you're between jobs, freelancing, or just starting out, you still have options. That's where government programs and marketplace plans come in.

Explore the Health Insurance Marketplace

Head to HealthCare.gov to shop for health insurance plans through the Affordable Care Act (ACA). Each year during Open Enrollment (typically from November to January), you can compare plans based on coverage, monthly premiums, deductibles, and out-of-pocket costs. If you've had a major life change, like losing a job, turning 26, aging out of your parents' plan, or moving, you may qualify for Special Enrollment outside of that window.

See If You Qualify for Medicaid

Medicaid is a government-funded, free or low-cost insurance program designed for individuals with limited income. Eligibility varies by state, so check your state's Medicaid website or HealthCare.gov to see if you qualify. If you're under a certain income level, this could be your best option.

Budget-Friendly Tips

When choosing a plan, think beyond the monthly premium. A low-cost plan might have a high deductible, meaning you'll pay more out of pocket if you need care. Look at your typical health needs and choose a plan that makes sense for your lifestyle, such as if you need regular prescriptions or have ongoing conditions.

No matter your situation, having health insurance helps protect you from huge medical bills and gives you access to preventive care. So even if you're young and healthy, it's worth making sure you're covered.

Renters and Homeowners Insurance: Because Your Stuff Won't Protect Itself

As a young adult, you're likely moving into your first apartment or house, and while insurance might not be top of mind, having renters' or homeowners' insurance is a wise move.

Renters Insurance covers your personal belongings in case of theft, fire, or other disasters. If you live in an apartment, there could be a fire, and you want to make sure your personal belongings are covered. Even if you don't think you own much, it's easy to overlook how quickly your possessions can add up in value. Renters' insurance also provides liability coverage if someone gets hurt in your rented space.

If you're buying a home, homeowners' insurance is essential. It covers your home's structure, your belongings, and liability if someone gets hurt on your property. Some lenders require homeowners' insurance, but even if it's not mandatory, it's a good idea to have it to protect your investment.

Real-Life Story: Why Renters Insurance Matters

When my brother and I rented an apartment together years ago, we had front-row seats to what happens when you don't have renters' insurance. One night, our downstairs neighbors thought it was cute to set the mood with a candle. Harmless, right? Wrong. That little candle decided it wanted to be a whole bonfire, and next thing you know, their entire apartment was up in flames.

Luckily, everyone made it out safe. But when the smoke cleared, they had *nothing.* Clothes? Gone. Furniture? Toast. TV, dishes, the kids' toys? All gone. And because they didn't have renters' insurance, there was no magic check coming in the mail to help them start over. They had to lean on the Red Cross, family, and friends just to scrape together basics like clothes and a mattress. Starting over came straight out of their own pockets, and let me tell you, it wasn't cheap.

That was the wake-up call for me. Renters insurance isn't just some "optional extra" your landlord casually mentions like it's Wi-Fi. It's the difference between bouncing back and being broke. For less than what you spend on Netflix, Hulu, *and* DoorDash in a month, you can protect all your personal belongings, your bed, your couch, and your sneakers.

Nobody ever thinks their apartment will catch fire, but life doesn't care what you think. Candles tip, kitchens burn, pipes burst. And when it does? You'll either be thanking yourself for that $15-a-month policy... or crying in the corner of your cousin's living room, trying to figure out how you're going to replace a whole apartment's worth of stuff. Your choice.

Additional Coverage Options: Travel and Pet Insurance

Once you've handled the "grown-up starter pack" of insurance, health, car, renters'/home, and maybe life, you might think you're done. But life always finds a way to throw a monkey wrench in your game, so there are a few extra types of coverage worth knowing about. These aren't for everyone, but for some people, they can be the difference between a manageable headache and a full-blown financial meltdown.

Travel Insurance might sound like something only nervous fliers or globe-trotting retirees bother with, but it's actually a lifesaver if you travel often—or even just once for that big, expensive trip you've been planning. Here's the deal: travel is unpredictable. Flights get canceled, luggage goes on a vacation of its own, and sometimes, you catch the flu the day before your flight. Travel insurance can reimburse you for trip cancellations, cover lost or delayed baggage, and even help with medical emergencies abroad (because I'm sorry to tell you, but your regular health insurance probably won't cover you in another country). Imagine breaking an ankle while zip-lining in Costa Rica—without travel insurance, you're paying out of pocket. With it, you can focus on healing instead of crying over the hospital bill.

Pet Insurance might sound extra bougie at first—like, really, we're insuring Fluffy now? But if you've ever owned a pet, you know they're basically furry toddlers who love to get into trouble. One random accident or health scare can rack up vet bills faster than you can say "ouch." Pet insurance helps cover those expensive visits, surgeries, and medications. Instead of choosing between paying your rent or saving your dog, you'll have a cushion to fall back on. And considering how much we treat our pets like family (yes, some of us throw them birthday parties), it just makes sense to make sure their health emergencies don't wreck your finances.

The bottom line is that travel and pet insurance may not be on the must-have list for everyone, but if you're a frequent flyer or a proud pet parent, they can save you from some major financial stress. Because let's face it, whether it's your suitcase vanishing in Paris or your cat deciding to swallow a shoelace, life doesn't care if you're "on a budget."

Final Thought

Nobody wakes up excited to shop for insurance, like "Ooooh, let me compare premiums today!" said no one ever. But taking the time to actually understand what you're signing up for and picking the right policies, that's grown-up gold. It's giving "I've got my life together," even if you still eat cereal for dinner sometimes.

Insurance is your financial seatbelt. You hope you never need it, but when life decides to act up, because it *will*, you'll be glad you buckled up. So go ahead, protect your stuff, your health, your future...and your peace of mind. Because when life goes left, the last thing you need is to be broke *and* stressed.

9

"I Got Car Money, Fresh Start Money, I Want Saudi Money, I Want Art Money" ~ Drake

Keys Please: Your First Ride Comes With Receipts

In the song *Dreams Money Can Buy*, Drake raps about "car money" and "fresh start money" as symbols of progress—the feeling that buying a car means you've reached a new level of independence. A car represents freedom, adulthood, and finally moving on your own schedule. What the line doesn't highlight, though, is everything that comes after the keys are in your hand. Because a car isn't just a fresh start; it's a long-term financial commitment that comes with monthly payments, insurance, maintenance, repairs, and surprise expenses nobody ever mentions. The freedom is real—but so are the receipts.

Let me tell you about my first car. I was a senior in high school, and my mom had finally had it with being my personal Uber driver. One day, she hit me with the classic "If you get your license, I'll buy you a car." Say less, Mom. You've never seen anyone move faster. I booked my road test so quickly her head spun, and within 30 days, I had that license in hand like it was a golden ticket.

I'm from New York, so parallel parking and backing into tight spaces is child's play for me. I could wedge an SUV into a spot meant for a moped. I passed on the first try and landed my first car: an Audi 5000. And listen, at 18, with my little part-time job and fresh license, I *was that girl!* Until the first repair bill hit. Nobody warned me that fixing an Audi costs more than the car was worth. That was my crash course in grown-up car ownership. Cute car, expensive lesson.

Buying your first car is exciting, but let's be real, it's not just about the wheels; it's about the bills. Whether you're buying new or used, or debating between cash and credit, the key is to go in with your eyes open and your wallet protected. So let's break it all the way down.

Buying New: The Pros, The Cons, and the Truth

So you're thinking about buying a brand-new car? It smells amazing, everything works, and it comes with the peace of mind that nobody else has been in that driver's seat. Sounds perfect, right? Well...kinda.

What's So Great About a New Car?

- Warranty Heaven: New cars usually come with a manufac-turer's warranty that covers most repairs for 3 to 5 years (sometimes longer). That means no sweating, surprise breakdowns, or paying out of pocket for big repairs right away.

- Low Maintenance (at First): Basic maintenance like oil changes and tire rotations might even be included. Less stress, less mess.
- All the Tech and Safety Perks: We're talking lane departure warnings, backup cameras, Bluetooth everything, and touchscreen dashboards. If you want the bells and whistles, a new car has them.
- Reliability: New means fewer chances of something going wrong, at least for the first few years. You won't have to guess how the last owner treated it either.

But Hold Up Here's the Flip Side

- Depreciation is a Beast: The second you drive that shiny car off the lot, it loses value. Like instantly. In the first year, you might lose twenty percent of what you paid. In five years, try sixty percent.
- It's Expensive: New cars come with a fat sticker price. Add taxes, registration fees, and insurance (which costs more for new cars), and your bank account will definitely feel it.
- Financing Comes With Baggage: Most young adults take out a car loan, which sounds cool until you realize you're stuck with monthly payments for the next 5–7 years. And if something changes, like losing your job or taking on other bills, those payments can feel like a financial chokehold.
- You Might Be "Upside Down": That's when you owe more on the car than it's worth. So, if you crash the car in an accident and total it or try to sell it early, good luck.

So, Is Buying New Worth It?

Depends on what lane you're in. If you want that shiny, never-been-driven ride with all the fancy gadgets, cool, but only if your bank account can actually keep up. Don't be out here riding clean while your fridge is empty and your savings account is crying. Buying new only makes sense if you can swing the payments, still save some money, and plan to keep that car until the wheels basically fall off. If that's your plan, go for it. But if not? There's zero shame in sliding into a used car. I bought my last car used when it was less than a year old, and now, it's paid off in full. I still think about a new car sometimes, sure, but do I really want a monthly payment that feels like I'm financing a small house? Nope. I'd rather keep my budget intact, have money for fun, and sleep at night knowing my car isn't bleeding my bank account dry. Trust me, your wallet (and your sanity) will thank you.

Gap Insurance: Don't Get Caught in the "Uh-Oh" Zone

So, you finally got the keys to your new (or new-to-you) car, congrats! But before you blast your victory playlist and hit the road, let's talk about a little something called gap insurance. It's not sexy, but it is smart.

What Is Gap Insurance?

Gap insurance stands for "Guaranteed Asset Protection." It covers the gap between what your car is worth and what you still owe on your loan or lease if your car gets totaled or stolen. Here's the tea: Cars start losing value the minute you drive them off the lot. That means in the first year or two, your loan might still be higher than the car's actual value.

Why You Might Need It

Let's say you bought a car for $25,000 and a year later it gets totaled. Your insurance company might only pay out $18,000 (based on the car's current value). But if you still owe $22,000 on your loan, you're on the hook for the $4,000 difference, unless you have gap insurance. Gap insurance swoops in and covers that $4K, so you're not paying for a car you can't even drive anymore.

You should think about getting gap insurance if:

- You financed most (or all) of your car with a loan or lease.
- You put down a small down payment (less than 20%).
- Your loan term is longer than 4 years.
- You're driving a car that depreciates quickly.

My Story: The Tree, the Temp Tags, and the Lifesaver Called Gap Insurance

Let me tell you about the time I bought a brand-new car and six weeks later, Mother Nature tried to ruin my life.

It was my first time buying a brand-new car; every car before that had been pre-owned. This one was fresh off the lot, sleek, shiny, and all mine. I was hyped. The dealership offered me gap insurance during the paperwork shuffle, and honestly, I almost said no. But something told me to add it just in case.

Six weeks later, while I was out of town on vacation, a winter storm rolled in and hit harder than anyone expected. I had left my car parked at a friend's house, thinking it would be safe. Then I got the call during the storm, a huge tree had snapped and crashed right onto my car. Crushed. Totaled. Temp tags were still on my car.

I called my insurance company, and they gave me the bad news: yes, they'd pay for the current market value of the car, but that wasn't enough to cover the full loan I had just taken out. Without gap insurance, I would've had to come out of pocket for the difference. Thousands of dollars for a car I couldn't even drive anymore, and only owned for six weeks.

But because I had bought gap insurance, that balance was covered. Every single dollar. I didn't owe anything on a car that was now a tree sandwich.

Moral of the story? Gap insurance saved me from a major financial disaster. It's one of those things you hope you never need...until you do.

I said all of that to say, if you'd rather not risk writing checks for a car you no longer have, gap insurance is a small price to pay for peace of mind.

Not Brand New, But Still a Blessing: The Used Car Game

We all want that shiny new ride with the dealer's fresh paint smell and zero miles on the odometer. But unless you're swimming in cash or your dad just hooked you up, buying new is usually a recipe for instant financial regret. Enter: the used car. Yes, it's not brand spanking new, but it's still a blessing, especially if your wallet's looking sad and empty.

First up, the obvious: used cars cost way less. Like shockingly less. You could either save that money for things like rent bills, or you know, actual adult stuff, *or* you could snag an older, fancier model, think luxury or SUV that you'd never afford new. It's like tricking the system, but legal.

And here's the kicker: new cars lose value faster than your patience at the DMV. We're talking a brutal twenty percent drop in the first year alone. Buy used, and you dodge that sucker punch. The car already lost its "new car" street cred, so it won't lose much more. Resell it later, and you won't cry over how much you lost. Financially, it's a smarter move if you can stomach the quirks.

Speaking of perks, insurance on used cars tends to be cheaper. Insurers don't like to shell out big bucks for older rides, so they charge you less. Bonus for the young and broke who are already paying through the nose for insurance coverage.

But hold up, before you run off to buy that sweet, slightly beat-up beauty, know this: older cars love drama. Repairs will come knocking like an annoying ex. And if you picked that "fancy European" used car because it looked cool on Instagram, hello Audi 5000 flashbacks, brace yourself for pricey maintenance that'll eat up those "savings." The "cheap" sticker price might disappear faster than your paycheck once those repair bills roll in.

Oh, and warranties? Forget about it. Most used cars come with about as much coverage as your last Tinder date's "commitment." Private sellers and sketchy dealerships don't throw in warranties. So, when stuff breaks, it's all on you, buddy. Some "Certified Pre-Owned" cars throw you a bone with limited warranties, but don't expect a miracle.

And just when you think you're done, here's the best part: car history reports are like trusting gossip from that shady cousin. Yeah, services like Carfax exist, but some sellers are pros at hiding skeletons, accidents, flood damage, or skipped maintenance like it's no big deal. Moral of the story? Don't just take their word. Do your homework like it's a final exam.

So, what's the survival guide? Step one: Take your soon-to-be car to a trusted mechanic for a full-on CSI investigation before you sign anything. That test drive doesn't reveal everything, so get someone who knows their stuff to check the engine, brakes, and whatever else might randomly decide to break. Step two: dive deep into that vehicle history report and look for red flags like a salvage title or car hopping owners like it's a hot potato. Step three: save some money for inevitable repairs because, yes, even "reliable" used cars still want oil changes and new tires.

Bottom line: buying used isn't a free pass to stress-free driving, but if you come in prepared and keep your eyes open, it's a pretty savvy move for anyone who'd rather spend their money on literally anything else.

Paying for Your Car: Cash or Financing?

Now that you've *decided* on a car that doesn't require selling a kidney, it's time for the ultimate adult dilemma: do you pay cash or finance? Spoiler alert: there's no "right" answer, just a lot of math and soul-searching.

Paying in Full (Cash)

If you've actually managed to save up enough cash to buy your car outright, congrats, you're the adult everyone wants to be. Paying cash means no monthly payments, no interest piling up like laundry, and no one breathing down your neck about late bills. The car is yours 100% free and clear. Plus, insurance might actually cost less because you don't owe the bank a dime.

But here's the catch: don't blow your entire savings on your new ride and then cry when your refrigerator breaks or you get hit with a surprise medical bill. Having zero backup funds because you paid cash is basically adulting gone wrong. Also, your cash budget might mean settling for that 2005 sedan with a questionable smell instead of your dream Tesla. Sacrifices.

Financing (Loan)

For most of us, not swimming in savings, financing is the practical route. Spread those payments out, keep your budget manageable, and maybe even score a better car than your cash stash would allow. Plus, if you actually pay on time, you get to build that all-important credit score, which you'll need when you want to buy a house, a fancy phone, or another car someday.

But (there's always a but) interest is the ultimate party pooper. You'll pay more than the car's worth over time because banks aren't charity organizations. The longer your loan, the more you pay, sometimes way more. Miss a payment? Say goodbye to your credit score and hello to angry calls from your lender. Worst case, your car gets repossessed and you're stuck with nothing but regret and a dent in your wallet.

Choosing What's Best for You

So what's the move? If you're sitting on enough cash to buy the car without turning broke and desperate, paying cash is the way to dodge debt drama. If you need a ride ASAP or want something nicer than what your cash covers, financing can be your friend if you're responsible enough to handle the payments.

If you finance, don't just grab the first loan the dealer waves in your face. That "special offer" they're hyping up? Yeah, it usually means it's *special for them*, not you. Always shop around. Your own bank or credit union will often give you lower auto loan rates than the dealership because they're not trying to squeeze every dime out of you. Credit unions, especially, are like the chill cousin in the family, less flashy, but way more on your side when it comes to money. Compare what they offer with your bank and even those sketchy-looking online lenders (but read the fine print before you sell your soul).

Here's the deal: shorter loans mean less interest overall, but higher monthly payments. Longer loans feel easier on your wallet each month, but you'll end up paying way more in the long run. So, pick your poison carefully. And whatever you do, don't let your car note turn your budget into a circus act where you're juggling bills and side hustles just to keep up. The car should take you places, not take over your life.

Negotiating the Best Deal: Hustle Hard Save Harder

Look, whether you're eyeing that shiny new ride or a "gently loved" used one, negotiating the price isn't just some optional flex; it's the only way to keep your pockets from crying. And no, just asking "Can you do better?" isn't enough. You have to come prepared like you're bargaining for your life (because you kinda are).

Don't Get Played at the Lot: Know Your Car's Real Worth

Before you roll up to the dealership or slide into a seller's DMs like, *"Hey, is this still available?"*, do your homework. You need to know what that car is actually worth, not what the seller swears it's worth, not what the sticker screams, and definitely not what your cousin's friend "who knows cars" claims.

That's where your new besties come in: Kelley Blue Book, Edmunds, and TrueCar. Think of these sites as your receipts, your armor, and your "don't try me" energy at the negotiation table. They'll give you real numbers based on the car's make, model, year, mileage, and condition. No sugarcoating, no fairy tales, just straight-up market value.

Here's how to use them:

- **Kelley Blue Book (KBB):** The OG. It gives you a range for trade-in, private party, and retail value, so you can see what the car's worth from every angle.
- **Edmunds:** This one's like KBB's detail-oriented cousin. It factors in regional pricing trends and even dealer incentives, so you know the bigger picture.
- **TrueCar:** Great if you hate awkward haggling. It shows you what people in your area actually paid for the same car, so you know whether that "deal" in front of you is really a deal or just dealership smoke and mirrors.

Let me give you an example: Say you've got your eye on a 2018 Honda Accord. The dealer hits you with, *"$20,000, it's a great deal!"* But before you whip out your pen, you check KBB and see it's worth around $16,500 in good condition. Edmunds shows you the average price in your area is about $17,200, and TrueCar proves folks nearby just bought the same model for $17K flat. Now you've got the ammo to walk back in and say, *"Actually, the market says this car is worth closer to $17K, so let's talk real numbers."*

That's a $3,000 swing just from five minutes of homework. And the difference between being taken for a ride and driving off with a solid deal is knowing where the market really stands. Salespeople can smell when you come prepared, and that's when the negotiating power shifts right into your hands.

Bottom line: Knowledge is power. And when it comes to car buying, it can also save you thousands of dollars and a whole lot of regret.

Be Ready to Bounce

Don't be that person who falls in love with a car before you even sign paper. If the dealer or seller isn't willing to meet your price, dust yourself off and walk away like you just dropped a mic. They'll probably call you back later with a sweeter deal because nobody likes watching a potential sale walk out the door.

Throw in Some Extras

If the price isn't budging, don't sweat it. Ask for freebies instead. Free oil changes, longer warranties, lower financing rates, whatever makes that deal look less like a trap and more like a steal. Sometimes the extras add up to more cash saved than the price drop you wanted anyway.

There's a Right Time to Buy a New Car

Buy a car right at the end of the month, quarter, or year. That's when dealers are sweating bullets to hit their sales goals. Picture this: every salesperson has a quota, and the manager is breathing down their neck to move just a few more cars to unlock bonuses. If you walk in at the right time, you're basically their golden ticket, and that means they might be way more willing to cut you a deal just to get one more sale on the books.

And it's not just about quotas. Timing lines up with the car industry's natural cycle. When the new models drop (usually late summer into fall), last year's cars suddenly look a little less shiny on the lot. Dealers want them gone, fast, so they'll start slashing prices or offering "incentives" like zero-interest financing or cashback just to clear space.

Don't sleep on holiday sales either. Memorial Day, Labor Day, Black Friday, even New Year's, they're like the Super Bowl of car shopping. Why? Because dealerships know people are out shopping, and they bait the hook with "event pricing." Some of it is hype, but a lot of the discounts are real, especially if you're strategic and show up ready to negotiate.

Moral of the story: when you buy can be just as important as what you buy. Pull up at the right time, and you're not just shopping, you're flipping the script on who's got the upper hand.

Get Pre-Approved and Level Up Your Negotiation

If financing, get pre-approved for a loan before you walk in. It tells the dealer, "Yeah, I'm serious and I know what I can afford." No more of that sneaky upsell nonsense, trying to get you into a loan you can't handle.

Negotiating feels like a headache, but it's your money, so don't let anyone play you. Know your limits, stick to your guns, and walk away with a deal that won't leave you struggling to pay the monthly car note.

Other Costs to Consider: Because The Sticker Price Isn't the Whole Story

Buying a car isn't just about the sticker price; it's about all those sneaky extras that pop up once you sign the papers. Insurance, maintenance, registration fees, the list goes on and on, and your wallet's going to feel it if you ignore these.

Insurance: Your Wallet's Arch-Nemesis

Young drivers, brace yourselves, insurance rates are basically designed to punish you for being young. Are you under 25? Welcome to the club where premiums are sky-high because apparently having fun and making mistakes means you're a financial risk. If you keep a clean record, though, and after 25, those premiums start to drop a little. Also, if you're rolling in a flashy sports car or a luxury SUV, expect to pay even more just for the "privilege" of driving it.

Your zip code, driving history, and credit score play into this mess, too. City drivers pay more because, surprise, more accidents happen in crowded places. And if your credit's bad? Insurance companies will hike your rates like you're a danger to society. So, make sure to find out how much the insurance will be on that car you're eyeing, and make sure you can afford it before you purchase it.

Maintenance and Repairs: The Never-Ending Story

That "new car smell" fades fast when you start paying for oil changes, new tires, and brakes. Sure, a brand-new ride usually gives you a honeymoon phase, no oil changes, no random dashboard lights screaming at you, but that won't last forever. Sooner or later, you're shelling out for tires, brakes, and all the other not-so-glamorous stuff that keeps your car alive.

Now, let's talk about used or older cars. They might save you money up front, but don't get it twisted, they're like ticking time bombs for your wallet. One minute you're cruising, the next you're on a first-name basis with your mechanic. And if you went the "I want to look fancy" route and grabbed a European car, those repairs will drain your account faster than you can say "luxury." Know what you're getting into and make sure you can maintain the maintenance on the car you choose.

Registration and Taxes: DMV's Favorite Cash Grab

Don't forget, your state's DMV wants its cut too. Registration fees vary depending on where you live, how big your car is, or how new it is, because apparently owning a nice car means you're rich enough to pay extra taxes. Sales tax on the purchase is another chunk of change dealers slide into the final bill without blinking. Buying from a private seller doesn't make you exempt from paying sales tax; you'll still have to pay up when you register the car at the DMV.

Want to know what you're really getting into? Hit up Edmunds.com, they've got the dirt on average insurance costs, maintenance schedules, car reviews, and registration fees for whatever car you're eyeballing because nothing says "adult" like budgeting for all the stuff that isn't the car itself.

Final Thought

Whether you decide to buy new, used, or "needs a prayer and a jump start," take your sweet time when it comes to deciding which route you're going to take when purchasing your first car. Ask the dumb questions, double-check everything, and plan for those inevitable "check engine" lights that show up like uninvited party crashers, usually right after payday.

Your car should get you where you're going without sending you into a financial spiral. Play it smart: reliable, affordable, and drama-free. Because nothing kills your new-car buzz faster than realizing your monthly car note payment is almost as high as your rent.

10

"I Need A Vacation! I'm Going to Decatur, Where It's Greater ~ Jeezy

The World Is Bigger Than Your Block

No, really. *There's life outside your city limits.* In the song *Vacation*, Jeezy talks about needing a break and heading somewhere familiar just to breathe, and what he's really speaking to is the urge to escape routine. Sometimes getting away doesn't mean hopping on a plane to somewhere exotic—it simply means stepping outside the same streets, habits, and mindset you see every day. That idea matters, especially when adulthood starts to feel like an endless loop of work, bills, and responsibilities tied to one zip code. Taking a break, even a small one, can shift your perspective and remind you that life exists beyond the routine you're stuck in.

Just because you've officially entered adulthood doesn't mean you're sentenced to a lifetime of work, sleep, repeat in the same place where you learned the Cha-Cha Slide. Being grown means you now have choices. You can explore new cities, experience different cultures, and realize there's more to life than the block you grew up on. And yes, that might start with a short trip somewhere close, but it can grow into passports, stamps, and seeing the world on your own terms. So pack your bags, Boo. The block will be just fine while you go remind yourself how big the world really is.

Whether you're fantasizing about sipping fresh coconut water on a beach in Jamaica, pretending you're in a rom-com (Romantic Comedy for the GenZers) while standing by the Eiffel Tower in Paris, or just road-tripping to the next state to eat food you didn't have to cook, travel is for you. Yup, even on a budget. Especially on a budget.

Back in the day, it felt like international trips were reserved for rich kids with country club parents. I'd see my neighbors rolling their Samsonite luggage into their SUVs every few months like it was their birthright. My friends would come back with the most amazing stories, and I knew then that it was something I wanted to do when I became an adult. Meanwhile, I was just trying to finesse a ride to Six Flags. But now, I'm the one with TSA PreCheck and a carry-on so light it floats. The world got bigger, and so did my ambition. And yours can too.

I've made it my mission to collect passport stamps, not just PTO hours. I used to think traveling was for people with trust funds; turns out it's actually for people with Google, patience, and a little strategy. I've checked off several countries so far (and trust, I'm just getting started), and now I'm giving you the blueprint so you can globe-trot too without going broke or sleeping on your cousin's air mattress in the process.

Passport to the Streets: Get Ya Papers Right So You Can Take Flight

So, you've been daydreamin' about dipping out to Bali, brunchin' in Italy, or flexin' in front of Big Ben for the 'Gram, cute. But baby, you can't even book the flight if you don't have your passport. That little navy-blue booklet is your golden ticket to the rest of the world. And trust nothing humbles you faster than finding out you can't join the squad's group trip because your paperwork isn't in order. Let's break it down step by step:

Step 1: Gather the docs you're going to need:

- Your original birth certificate or proof of U.S. citizenship (not a photocopy—the real deal). Since your original birth certificate will be sent in with your application, be sure to make a photocopy for your records, just in case you need it before it's returned to you.
- A valid government-issued photo ID (your driver's license or government-issued ID).
- A passport photo (taken within the last 6 months, no filters, no Snapchat bunny ears). Most CVS, Walgreens, or USPS stores take passport photos for around $15. No selfies allowed, sorry, not this time.

Step 2: Fill Out the Application:

- You'll need to complete Form DS-11 if you're getting your first passport. You can fill it out online and print it or grab a paper copy at a passport acceptance facility (usually the post office). DO NOT sign the form until you're in front of the passport agent, or they'll hit you with the "try again" face.

Step 3: Make That Appointment:

· Go to <u>travel.state.gov</u> to find a passport acceptance facility near you (post offices, clerk of court offices, etc.). Many locations require an appointment, especially since the world is traveling again. Don't just show up on a random Tuesday; set up an appointment.

Step 4: Pay Up, Buttercup. Here's what it'll cost you:

· Passport book (for international air travel): $130
· Execution fee (aka the handling cost): $35
· Total regular cost: $165
· Expedited service (optional): +$60
· Total expedited: $225 (if you're in a hurry)

You'll usually pay with a check or money order for the passport itself ($135) and a separate form of payment (like a debit card) for the $35 execution fee. Don't act surprised, they don't take CashApp or Apple Pay.

Step 5: The Waiting Game:

· Routine processing: 6 to 8 weeks.
· Expedited: About 2 to 3 weeks.
· Life-or-death emergency: There's a special process for that, but it better be real. Not "I forgot my cousin's wedding

is in Cancun next weekend" energy.

Once your passport comes in the mail, guard it with your life. Lock it up, scan a copy, and never flex it in public. The last thing you want is to lose your passport or have it stolen.

Bottom Line: No passport = no international moves. So stop playing and handle that paperwork. Your future jet-setting self will thank you.

My Story: The $247 Dubai Trip That Got Away

A few years ago, I came across what felt like the travel deal of a lifetime: a glitch in the Emirates Airline system had round-trip tickets to Dubai for just $247. My girlfriend and I jumped on it instantly, booked our seats, and were already daydreaming about desert safaris and rooftop views.

There was just one little problem: I didn't have a passport. I figured, no big deal, I'd apply right away and still have plenty of time before the trip. But when I submitted my application, everything went sideways. At the time, I had just moved from Los Angeles to Maryland. My driver's license still showed my California address, but my application listed my new Maryland address. That mismatch set off red flags. Suddenly, the State Department thought my application might be fraudulent.

What should have been a straightforward 6–8 week process turned into a four-month ordeal. I had to gather and submit multiple pieces of documentation just to prove I was really me. Meanwhile, the clock kept ticking.

By the time my passport finally arrived, the plane to Dubai had long taken off, without me on it. My girlfriend, who booked her ticket alongside mine, still went and had the adventure we'd planned together, while I stayed home scrolling through her Instagram posts with serious FOMO.

Lesson learned: When it comes to travel, have all your paperwork in order before you book. A good deal means nothing if you can't actually get on the plane.

Flight Hacking 101: Cheap Flights Rich Kid Vibes

If you've ever spent hours scrolling through travel sites, crying over how expensive flights are, Google Flights Explore is about to become your new BFF. It's basically a map of the world with prices plastered all over it, letting you see where you can go without selling a kidney. You don't have to commit to one destination; you can just let the cheap flights tell you where to dip. It shows real prices from airlines (no shady hidden fees buried in fine print), lets you compare dates, and even tracks price drops so you don't miss a deal. Translation: you're shopping smart, not broke.

How to Use Google Flights Explore to Snag Cheap Trips

1. Pull up Google Flights - Type "Google Flights" into your search bar. Boom. No secret handshake needed.
2. Hit "Explore" - At the top, there's a tab that says "Explore." Click it. Don't overthink.
3. Choose Your Departure Spot - Put in your home airport. If you've got multiple airports nearby, throw them all in; sometimes that little drive can save you hundreds.
4. Leave the Destination Blank (Trust Me) - The magic happens when you don't lock yourself into one place. Keep it open and let the cheap flights tell you where you're going.

5. Pick Dates or Stay Flexible - If you got PTO approved, lock in your dates. If you're just trying to dip whenever the price is right, use the flexible option like "1 week in December" or "Weekend in March."

6. Filter the Nonsense - Nobody's trying to spend 27 hours in an airport with two layovers in random cities. Use the filters for "nonstop," airlines, and bags so you don't get played.

7. Zoom Around the Map - This is the fun part. Slide the map around and watch prices pop up over different cities. You'll see deals you never even thought about.

8. Click the Deal - See a flight you like? Click it. You'll get the breakdown of times, airlines, and what you're really paying for.

9. Turn On Price Tracking - Not ready to commit? Hit that "Track prices" button so Google can snitch on the airlines for you and send an alert when prices drop.

10. Book That Trip - Once you find your deal, book it directly through the airline or site Google kicks you to. Congrats, you just played the system like a champ.

Pro Tips to Score Even Cheaper Flights

- Fly Midweek: Tuesdays and Wednesdays usually have lower fares than Fridays or Sundays. Less demand = more savings.
- Red-Eye Flights: Late-night or super-early flights are less popular, so airlines often drop the price. Bonus: You might sleep through part of the travel.
- Shoulder Seasons: Traveling just before or after peak season (like early spring or late fall) gets you lower prices and smaller crowds.

- Be Flexible With Airports: Sometimes flying out of a nearby airport instead of your main one can save hundreds.
- Track Those Prices: Google Flights lets you track fares so you'll know exactly when to pounce—no guessing required.

Follow these tips, combine them with your Google Flights Explore map skills, and suddenly "affordable vacation" isn't a fantasy anymore, it's your new reality.

Other Websites and App Tools That Help You Save on Travel

- Sky Scanner – Use the "Everywhere" feature to find the cheapest country to run away to.
- Hopper – Tells you when to book or wait. Like a flight fortune teller.
- Going (formerly Scott's Cheap Flights) – Alerts you when flights drop so low, you feel like you're robbing the airline.
- The Flight Deal – Posts flash sales and error fares. Blink, and you'll miss 'em.
- Travel Pirates - curates deeply discounted flights, hotels, and vacation packages.
- CheapCaribbean - Great site for all-inclusive vacation steals and deals that include round-trip airfare.

Broke Today, Bora Bora Tomorrow: BNPL Travel

Have you ever found a flight deal that made your heart skip a beat, but your bank account was looking at you like, *"Try me if you want to."* That's where Buy Now, Pay Later (BNPL) services come in clutch. Apps like Affirm, Klarna, AfterPay, and websites like Airfordable and Uplift let you grab that ticket today and break the cost down into smaller, manageable payments. Instead of dropping $600 all at once, you might pay $150 every two weeks until it's covered. And just like that, you're booked without instantly blowing your whole paycheck.

But let's keep it all the way real: BNPL is not free money. If you miss payments, fees will eat you alive, and your "dream vacation" could quickly turn into a nightmare and collection calls. Think of it like training wheels, helpful, but not something you lean on forever. Use it wisely, and only if you've got a steady income to cover those future payments.

Now, here's another hack: buying one-way tickets each way. Instead of paying a fat lump sum for a round trip, spread out the cost. Buy your ticket *there* with this paycheck, then buy your ticket *back* with the next one. Airlines don't care if your flights are bought separately, and sometimes one-way tickets even come out cheaper than round-trip. Plus, if you're flexible, you can mix airlines to save even more, fly out on Delta, and come back on Southwest. Who said loyalty always pays?

Bottom line: Whether you're splitting your flight into payments with BNPL or splitting it into two one-way tickets, the goal is the same, get to your destination without draining your bank account or maxing out your credit card. Travel smart, so when you land, you've still got money for food, excursions, and maybe even a souvenir that isn't a refrigerator magnet.

Stack Points, Not Problems

You know that credit card sitting in your wallet doing nothing? It could be your ticket to your next destination if you play it right. Travel rewards cards give you points for everyday purchases like gas, groceries, and your bi-weekly Target run. Use those points to book flights, hotels, and more.

Some cards even give you massive sign-up bonuses, like enough points to get you halfway around the world *for free*. Just make sure you're not out here spending like Beyoncé with a DoorDash budget. Pay it off monthly. Don't let a trip to Cabo turn into a lifetime of credit card regret.

Travel Reward Credit Cards Worth Looking Into

- Chase Sapphire Preferred: This card is a favorite for travelers who want flexibility and big rewards. You earn points on travel and dining, and those points can be transferred to airline and hotel partners, giving you more value for your trips. It also comes with a generous sign-up bonus, which could cover a weekend getaway or a few flights if you hit the spending requirement early.
- Capital One Venture Rewards: If simplicity is your style, this card delivers. You earn unlimited miles on every purchase, and redeeming them for flights, hotels, or other travel expenses is straightforward—no complicated point systems to figure out. It's perfect for travelers who want flexibility without the hassle.
- American Express Gold or Delta SkyMiles: These cards cater to people who want extra perks while traveling. Amex Gold earns bonus points on dining and groceries, which can be converted into flights or hotels, plus it offers travel credits and perks for frequent flyers. Delta SkyMiles is tailored to loyal Delta travelers, with benefits like free checked bags, priority boarding, and faster mileage accumulation toward future trips.

Low-Effort Luxury: How to Earn Miles Without Booking a Flight

If you're going to spend money anyway, you might as well earn free flights while you're at it. That's the kind of grown-up multitasking we love. Several Airlines are getting in on the "Shop & Earn" Game:

- American Airlines eShopping (Chrome Extension = Game Changer): Install the American Airlines AAdvantage eShopping Chrome extension and boom, every time you shop online at hundreds of stores (think Macy's, Sephora, Nike, Walmart, even DoorDash) you'll earn AAdvantage miles just for clicking "add to cart." It's giving *low-effort luxury*. No plane, no passport, just points stacking in the background.
- Delta SkyMiles Shopping: Delta's got a similar setup. Sign up for SkyMiles Shopping and earn miles every time you buy from partner retailers like Apple, Adidas, and Best Buy. Bonus points for stacking it with a Delta credit card if you have one.
- United MileagePlus Shopping: Yes, even United is here for your retail therapy. With MileagePlus Shopping, you earn United miles at stores like Kohl's, Ulta, and Groupon. Check their site before you buy anything online; you might be one click away from a future vacation.
- Southwest Rapid Rewards Shopping: Southwest has its own Rapid Rewards Shopping portal where you can earn points at places like Sam's Club, Old Navy, and Home Depot. So yes, even buying a new mop could get you closer to Mexico.

Bonus: Eat Your Way to Free Flights

- American Airlines AAdvantage Dining
- Delta SkyMiles Dining
- United MileagePlus Dining
- Southwest Rapid Rewards Dining

These programs give you extra miles just for linking a debit or credit card and using it at participating restaurants. No punch cards, no apps. Just eat, pay, and collect those coins or miles.

For additional savings, use the shopping portal + airline credit card + store sale = triple win. For example, order Nike shoes through Delta SkyMiles Shopping, use a Delta Amex card, and catch a promo sale? That's miles on miles on miles.

Moral of the story: You don't have to be a jet-setter to rack up travel points. You just have to shop smart. Because if you're going to spend money anyway, you might as well let those purchases get you a free trip *somewhere with sun, sand, or at least free hotel slippers.*

Young, Broke, and Discounted

If you're under 26 or still riding the student wave, congrats, your age is a discount code. Sites like StudentUniverse and UNiDAYS offer flight deals, rail passes, and even discounted hostels. Don't let that student ID just gather dust; it's basically a passport to cheaper adventures.

Hostels, But Make It Cute

Hostels used to have a bad rap, like bunk beds and body odor. But they've evolved, honey. Many offer private rooms, rooftop bars, and even yoga classes. Apps like Hostelworld, Booking.com, and Airbnb will help you book something clean, cheap, and Instagrammable.

And if anyone tries to clown you for not staying at a resort? Let them. You'll be sipping mojitos in Spain while they're still trying to get PTO approved.

Checked Bag Fees Are the Devil: Pack Light or Pay the Price

Checked bag fees are straight-up robbery. Why pay $35 just so your suitcase can take a nap in the cargo hold? Save your money and pack smart.

First rule of budget travel: pack light and pack with intention. You do *not* need a whole wardrobe change for every hour of the day. Re-wear outfits. Mix and match. Nobody's checking for your outfit repeat unless you're Rihanna, and even she recycles looks sometimes.

Roll your clothes to save space (yes, it actually works). Or take it up a notch with vacuum-seal bags—they suck the air out of your clothes and the drama out of your packing.

Want to really level up? Bring solid toiletries (like lotion sticks and deodorant bars) so TSA doesn't hit you with the dreaded "excuse me, ma'am, step aside" energy. Plus, solids won't spill and ruin your one good outfit.

And let's talk shoes: you don't need six pairs for a five-day trip. This is a vacation, not Paris Fashion Week. Pick two or three versatile pairs and keep it pushing.

Pack smarter, not heavier—your back, your wallet, and your TSA line anxiety will thank you.

Do It for the Memories, Not Just the 'Gram

Skip overpriced tourist traps. Some of the best moments cost $0. Walk the city. Talk to locals. Eat street food. People-watch from a park bench. Use TripAdvisor, Meetup, and Viator to find free walking tours and events. Real travel isn't just curated Instagram content; it's about feeling alive in a new place.

Travel Insurance = Real Adult Business

The words "travel insurance" don't exactly scream excitement, but you know what else isn't exciting? Landing in Morocco and your suitcase pulling a Houdini. Or catching a stomach bug in Thailand that has you sprinting to the bathroom every 15 minutes with no help in sight. Adult moves mean planning for the best, but being ready for the worst. That's where travel insurance comes in.

You wouldn't buy a car and skip buying the car insurance, right? So why would you book an international trip, spending your hard-earned money, without protecting your investment? A few coins up front could save you hundreds, even thousands, later.

What Travel Insurance Covers (and Why You'll Be Glad You Had It):

- Trip Cancellation or Interruption: Flight got canceled? Family emergency back home? Missed your connection because

131

the airline couldn't get it together? Travel insurance helps you recoup those nonrefundable costs, so you're not out here eating the loss.

- Medical Emergencies: Your regular health insurance probably doesn't work overseas. If you twist an ankle zip-lining in Costa Rica or catch something funky from that street food in Bangkok, travel insurance can cover hospital visits, medication, or even emergency medical evacuation if things get really real.
- Lost, Stolen, or Delayed Luggage: You show up to vacation, but your bag takes a detour to Antarctica. Travel insurance helps cover the cost of replacing your essentials while the airline plays detective.
- Travel Delays: If your flight gets delayed overnight, travel insurance can reimburse you for food, lodging, and other expenses you didn't plan for because airport sleeping is not the move.
- Emergency Evacuation or Repatriation: Sounds dramatic, but if a natural disaster hits or political unrest breaks out, travel insurance can cover your safe ride home, and trust me, that's not cheap without it.

Some things to make sure of before you hit the checkout button:

- Look into providers like SafetyWing (great for digital no-mads and long-term travelers) or World Nomads (perfect for backpackers, adventure seekers, and regular travelers alike).
- Always read the fine print so you know exactly what's covered.
- Buy your insurance *before* your trip; you can't get coverage

for a disaster that's already happening.
- Many airlines offer travel insurance before you check out and buy your ticket.

Bottom line: don't leave home without it, especially when you're traveling internationally. Because while you might be good at rolling with the punches, you deserve to vacation in peace, not panic. This is grown-up travel, and grown-ups *stay* ready.

Get Inspired Then Get Gone

Don't wait until you're rich, married, retired, or whatever else you've convinced yourself has to come first. Follow travel creators, watch vlogs, and save travel TikToks for information about your intended destination. Search #cheapflights or #inexpensivetravel and fall down the rabbit hole. Plan your trip itinerary ahead of time so you can budget smartly. And just *go*.

Final Boarding Call: The World Is Yours

You don't need to be a millionaire to make memories across the globe. You just need a plan, some discipline, and a suitcase (preferably one with wheels that don't squeak). Start small if you have to. A road trip counts. A weekend getaway counts. A solo flight across the world? Oh, that counts *twice*.

So, get that passport. Book that ticket. Toast to new time zones and fresh perspectives. Because baby, the world is *so much* bigger than your block, and it's waiting on you.

"We Know The Pain is Real, But You Can't Heal What You Never Reveal" ~ Jay-Z

Don't Just Survive, Thrive: Creating a Life Beyond the 9-5

In the song *Kill Jay Z*, Jay-Z raps honestly about pain and the cost of pretending everything is fine. He's pointing out something many adults struggle with: showing up, handling responsibilities, and keeping life moving, even while quietly carrying stress, exhaustion, or unresolved issues. But pushing through without ever checking in with yourself doesn't make you strong; it just postpones the moment when everything catches up. Healing requires acknowledgment. You can't fix what you refuse to face, and ignoring what's really going on only allows it to take up more space later.

Welcome to one of adulting's biggest plot twists: trying to keep it together while low-key falling apart. Between chasing checks, juggling school or work, answering texts, and trying not to ghost your partner, it's easy to forget the one thing that matters most...YOU. This chapter is your official permission slip to slow down, breathe, and take care of your mental, physical, and emotional health, without feeling bad about it, because burnout isn't the goal.

Hustle Culture Ain't It

My generation, Gen X, grew up watching our Baby Boomer parents work nonstop sunup to sundown like rest was some kind of luxury they couldn't afford. Somewhere along the way, we picked up the idea that being constantly busy meant you were successful. But let's be honest, this whole "booked and busy" lifestyle starts to lose its shine when you're burnt out, underpaid, and running on nothing but iced coffee and anxiety.

That's why I genuinely respect how Gen Z has flipped the script. Y'all said *no thanks* to glorified hustle culture and *yes please,* to peace of mind. You're setting boundaries, quitting toxic jobs, doing yoga, and prioritizing your well-being over burnout. That's the energy we all need.

In this chapter, we're diving into how to protect your peace while still handling your grown-up responsibilities because surviving adulthood shouldn't mean sacrificing your sanity.

The Self-Care Starter Kit

Self-care extends beyond bubble baths and skincare, even though we enjoy them both. The practice of self-care involves establishing routines that maintain your stability during periods of chaos.

Build a Morning Routine That Puts You First (Yes, Even Before Scrolling TikTok)

Start your day by choosing *you*, yes, even before your phone, your boss, or that chaotic group chat. Spending just five to ten minutes doing something grounding (not doom-scrolling) can shift your whole mood. Think: saying a few affirmations, journaling, stretching, or sitting quietly meditating before life starts life-ing.

Personally, I have affirmations stuck to my bathroom mirror like Post-it pep talks. Every morning, I stand in front of the mirror and look myself in the eye (while still half-asleep, honestly) and say them out loud. It might seem small, but it helps set the tone before the day tries to snatch my peace.

Here's the thing: you don't need a 5 AM wake-up call, an hour-long routine, or a green smoothie made with hand-picked kale. Just do *one* thing that feeds your spirit and reminds you that you're in control, at least for the first five minutes of the day.

Joy Isn't a Luxury; It's a Life Requirement

Adulting can feel like a never-ending group project where you're doing all the work and still getting graded unfairly. That's why finding joy isn't just nice to have; it's essential. It's not some cute bonus you "earn" after ticking off a million to-dos.

You need to make time for things that bring you *life*, like playing pickleball, watching your favorite show, rewatching the same anime episode for the 3rd time, or laughing at memes without guilt. Yes, joy counts as productivity. Yes, binge-watching that series you love is self-care. Schedule your "joy breaks" like you would a Zoom call with your boss. Set a 20-

minute appointment with happiness and protect it like your Wi-Fi bill depends on it.

Move Your Body, Save Your Sanity

Your body and brain are on the same team—when one's off, the other usually follows. That doesn't mean you need to train for a triathlon or run a marathon. Start small, keep it fun, and find movement you actually enjoy. A brisk walk around the block or even pacing your apartment complex like you're late for something still counts. You can pull up a 10–30 minute YouTube workout to get your muscles moving, or sign up for a Zumba or dance class and laugh at yourself the whole time with friends. If you're feeling adventurous, try indoor rock climbing for a little thrill and some serious upper-body work. Or grab a paddle and give pickleball a shot—it's social, competitive, and easier on the knees than tennis.

And now for the most underrated flex of all time: SLEEP. Not "accidentally passed out while scrolling TikTok" sleep. We mean *real* sleep. Restorative knock-you-out, wake-up-feeling-refreshed sleep. Your body actually needs it to heal, recharge, and make better decisions (like not sending that risky text or spending your last $40 on DoorDash).

If falling asleep feels impossible, create a routine that tells your brain, "Hey, it's time to shut down." That could mean dimming the lights, turning off your phone (yes, I said it), or putting on some calming sleep affirmations on the Calm App or YouTube. Personally, I swear by those whispery, "you are safe, you are loved" videos; they hit different after a long day.

The bottom line is this: take care of yourself like you matter. Because you do. And no, you *cannot* pour from an empty cup, no matter how many iced coffees you chug.

Boundaries: I Said What I Said, Respectfully

Listen, if "inner peace" had a price tag, it would be worth more than your rent, student loans, and Wi-Fi bill *combined*. So let's talk boundaries because protecting your time, energy, and sanity is the ultimate form of self-respect.

You don't have to say "yes" just because someone asked nicely or loudly or sent a "u up?" text at 1:42 am. Whether it's that one friend who only hits you up when they're in a crisis (again), a coworker who *loves* to overshare, or that group chat that turns every hangout into a 12-hour mission, *you're allowed to say no.*

Your Time = Your Power

Start treating your time and energy like money in the bank. You wouldn't hand out $100 bills to everyone who walked by, right? So stop giving your time and emotional energy away like it's a clearance sale at Target. When your account's drained, you're the one stuck, overdrafted on sleep, peace, and patience.

Here are a few phrases to help you shut things down *without* burning bridges (unless you're into that kind of thing):

- "I can't commit to that right now." (Translation: I'm busy. Or I just don't feel like it.)
- "Let me get back to you." (Spoiler: you might not. And that's okay.)
- "Thanks for thinking of me, but I'm going to pass." (Polite, but still a no.)
- Or my personal favorite: just hit 'em with a confident, non-

negotiable **"No."**

Simple. Direct. No TED Talk required.

Saying No = Choosing You

Every time you say "nah, I'm good" to something that drains you, you're saying *yes* to yourself. That's real self-love, not bubble baths and face masks (though we love those too).

Setting boundaries doesn't make you mean, selfish, or "too much." It makes you someone who values their peace more than people-pleasing. And honestly? That's the kind of energy adulting *really* requires.

So, the next time someone tries to guilt-trip you into overextending yourself, just remember, you're not a vending machine. You don't have to be available 24/7. Period. Respectfully.

Mindfulness Isn't Just for Bald Dudes on a Mountain

Let's get one thing straight: you don't need to be perched on a mountaintop in a lotus pose humming "ommmm" to get your mind right. Mindfulness isn't reserved for monks or influencers who claim they've "healed their inner child" by drinking cucumber water and lighting sage in every room.

Being mindful just means being *present,* like actually paying attention to the moment you're in, instead of spiraling about your to-do list or replaying that one awkward thing you said five years ago. It's your brain's way of saying, "Hey, can we *not* have a full-on breakdown today?"

And guess what? It doesn't take a whole hour or some $200 meditation retreat in Tulum. It just takes a moment. Literally.

Just a moment to pause and say, *"Lemme get my life together real quick."*

Try These Low-Effort Mindfulness Hacks:

- Deep Breathing (Calm Down Before You Snap) Try the 4-4-4 method: inhale for 4 seconds, hold for 4 seconds, exhale for 4 seconds. Boom. You just tricked your brain into thinking you're calm, perfect for when your group chat is chaotic or your bank account is stressing you out.
- Progressive Muscle Relaxation (a fancy term for "stop clenching your jaw"). Tighten and release each muscle group from your toes to your forehead like you're slowly powering down. Feels weird at first, but your body will finally be like, "Thanks for letting me chill."
- Mindful Eating (a.k.a. Stop Inhaling Your Food Like Life Is a Race) Put the phone down, turn off Netflix, and actually taste your food. Yes, your lunch deserves your undivided attention, too. Even if it's just ramen noodles again.
- Gratitude Journaling (no, it's not corny, calm down) Write down three good things from your day. Like "I didn't cuss anyone out today" or "I remembered to drink water." Small wins still count. Gratitude keeps your mood in check.

These lil' habits may seem like background extras in the movie of your life, but over time they add up and suddenly you're less stressed, more focused, and not spiraling every time someone says "We need to talk."

Bottom line, mindfulness isn't about perfection; it's about awareness. So breathe, stretch, *let it go,* and give yourself permission to not have it all figured out 24/7.

Therapy: Because Sometimes Journaling Just Isn't Enough

Can we stop acting like going to therapy means you're broken? Because newsflash: *we all have baggage,* some of us are just out here trying to unpack it like grown folks.

Therapy isn't some last-ditch effort when you're on the verge of snapping. It's maintenance like getting your oil changed or cleaning out that scary drawer in the kitchen. It's a space where you can spill all the tea, *without* judgment, and actually get some useful feedback instead of "just stay positive" energy.

I see my therapist monthly. Sometimes we talk about stress from work or issues from old relationships, other times it's childhood trauma I thought I left back in 2004. Either way, it's a safe space where I can say "Life is life-ing today" and get real tools to deal with it.

And let's be honest, most of us are walking around reacting to stuff based on some unhealed version of ourselves. Therapy helps you *connect the dots,* break those toxic patterns, control your emotions, and stop blaming Mercury in retrograde for all your problems.

Are you ready to give therapy a try? Here's where to start: First, acknowledge that reaching out for help is a brave and important step; there's no shame in wanting help. Next, think about what kind of therapy might feel right for you: individual sessions, group therapy, or even online counseling. Do a little research on licensed therapists in your area or reputable tele-health platforms, read reviews, and check their specialties. Don't worry about finding the "perfect" therapist right away— sometimes it takes meeting a couple of people to find the right fit. Finally, permit yourself to prioritize this time for yourself.

Booking that first session is not just a date on a calendar—it's a commitment to your mental health and overall well-being. Here is a list of places you can start:

- Online sites like BetterHelp, Talkspace, or GrowTherapy – Talk to a real therapist from your phone or via Zoom while wearing your bonnet or gym shorts.
- School or Work Benefits – A lot of colleges and jobs offer free or discounted therapy, and people don't even realize it.
- Ask Around – Yep, referrals work here too. Your friend might know the exact therapist who'll listen to you *and* help you heal.

Contrary to popular belief, taking care of your mental health doesn't make you weak; it makes you smart and strong. Therapy is not just a choice, it's a *life upgrade.* So go ahead and book that session. Your peace of mind is worth way more than ignoring your issues and hoping they magically disappear.

My Story: Breakups, Breakdowns, and Breakthroughs

Let me keep it all the way real: I didn't go to therapy because I had some big "aha!" moment about healing or personal growth. Nope. I went because I had just crawled out of an almost four-year relationship that left me on emotional life support. You know the kind, can't eat, can't sleep, playlist stuck on nothing but sad love songs and Toni Braxton singing "Unbreak My Heart," and your brain won't stop hitting replay like it's trying to torture you on purpose.

At first, I was like, *"Okay, sis, chin up. We don't cry over men, we glow up, remember?"* I was ready to slap on some lip gloss and post a fire selfie with the caption "unbothered." But deep down, I *was* bothered. What I *thought* was just a regular-degular breakup turned out to be a whole crash course in emotional baggage I didn't even know I had.

The anxiety hit first. I couldn't sleep. I couldn't shut my mind off. I kept thinking about every fight, every moment I let things slide, every time I shrank myself to "keep the peace." And then it hit me, this wasn't just about *him*. This was about *me*.

Why was I always the one over-functioning in relationships? Why did I keep choosing emotionally unavailable men and then playing emotional contortionist just to be "good enough"? And why deep down did I not believe I deserved more?

That's when therapy walked in like *"Oh, hey sis, are you finally ready to unpack that trauma?"*

And let me tell you: the way that breakup dragged out childhood wounds like it had a search warrant. I wasn't ready. I learned that my real issue wasn't him leaving, it was me never feeling safe enough to *be me*. I realized I was the "cool girlfriend" in relationships because I thought staying quiet and never causing problems made me lovable. Plot twist: it made me resentful and invisible.

Oh, and him? He moved on to his next victim just *weeks* after we broke up, like nothing happened, like nothing was even wrong with *him*. Because it takes two to tango in a relationship, but he'll never tell that part of the story. I found out (thanks to therapy and late-night Googling) that he was an avoidant narcissist who used love bombing, gaslighting, and manipulation as his go-to strategies. Classic. He was set in his ways, emotionally unavailable, and completely incapable of accepting accountability and giving and receiving unconditional love. And through all my healing, I realized something major:

I was never really the problem. I could've shown up as the most perfect, peaceful, supportive version of myself, and he still would've found something wrong. Because when someone is committed to misunderstanding you, it doesn't matter how good you are, they'll never see it.

Turns out I wasn't heartbroken over *him*; I was grieving *myself*. The parts of me I buried. The boundaries I never set. The "yeses" I gave when I meant "hell no." The times I apologized for things I didn't even do wrong, just to keep the peace.

Therapy didn't wave a magic wand and fix me overnight. (I wish.) But it handed me the tools I didn't even know I needed. I learned that boundaries aren't rude, they're necessary. That anxiety isn't a personality trait. And that my worth isn't measured by who stays but by how well I choose *me*.

That breakup hurt like hell because I truly thought he was my person. We were so compatible in everything, or so I thought. But therapy taught me that what looked like compatibility and a soulmate was really trauma bonding. And the moment I stopped begging people to choose me and finally started choosing myself was the beginning of my becoming. I started pouring that energy back into me, learning what I liked, what I deserved, and what I would never tolerate again. That heartbreak didn't just break me; it rebuilt me into someone stronger, wiser, and in love with myself.

Choose Your People Wisely (Not Everyone Deserves a VIP Pass in Your Life)

Not everybody deserves front-row access to *you*. Just because someone's been around forever or you grew up together doesn't mean they still fit where you're going. Loyalty is cute and all, but not when it comes at the cost of your peace, sanity, or self-worth.

We've all had that one friend who's draining the life out of us like it's their full-time job. The one who only calls when *they* need something. The one who lowkey competes with you, throws subtle shade, or disappears when life stops being convenient for *them*. Yeah, them. Newsflash: that's not friendship. That's a situationship with a social title.

Here's the truth nobody tells you when you start adulting: your circle will shrink. And that's not a tragedy, that's a glow-up. Quality over quantity always.

You need people in your life who clap when you win, check you when you're slipping, and actually *show up* without being asked three times and sent a calendar invite. You deserve folks who celebrate your boundaries instead of guilt-tripping you for having them. If the people around you constantly leave you feeling drained, second-guessing yourself, or emotionally bankrupt, it's time to audit your circle like you're the IRS.

Ask yourself:

- Do they genuinely support me, or do they just tolerate me?
- Do I feel safe being my full self around them?
- Do they take accountability, or do they make excuses?

If the answer to any of those is a hard *no*, it might be time to let them go like expired milk. No shade, just facts.

Because here's what happens when you finally start choosing your people wisely: you attract folks who pour into you the way you've always poured into others. People who match your energy instead of draining it. People who aren't afraid of your growth but actually *cheer for it.*

Let this be your reminder: you are not obligated to keep relationships that are rooted in guilt, convenience, or history alone. You are allowed to evolve, and your relationships should evolve with you. If they don't, you're not being mean for walking away. You're just protecting your peace like it's a limited-edition drop. Choose wisely. Your energy isn't cheap, and access to you should be earned, not handed out like free samples.

What About Your Friends? How to Spot a Real One (aka Friendship Red & Green Flags)

Real friends are **consistent,** not just convenient. If someone only pops up when it benefits them, congrats, you don't have a friend, you've got a seasonal associate. You deserve better than someone who treats your life like a revolving door.

Here's how to determine who's really a good friend to you:

They respect your boundaries. A real friend is someone who won't catch an attitude when you say "no." They won't guilt-trip you for needing space or time to yourself; they honor it, no questions asked.

They give you energy, not drain it. If you need a whole week-end to recover every time y'all hang out, that's not friendship, that's emotional exhaustion disguised as loyalty. Being around your people should leave you feeling lighter, not like you just ran a mental marathon.

They support your growth, not just your comfort zone. If somebody starts getting shady when you level up, that's not love, that's low-key jealousy. Don't shrink to make insecure people feel tall. Your shine should inspire them, not threaten them.

And let's not forget they actually listen. If every conversation turns into their personal TED Talk and you're always fighting to get a word in, you're not building a friendship, you're working overtime as their unpaid therapist.

Here's the bottom line: if you constantly feel like you're walking on eggshells, questioning your worth, or dimming your light to keep someone else from feeling insecure, that isn't your person. That's an energy leak. And guess what? You're allowed to patch the hole and walk away. Protect your peace, it's priceless.

My Story: From 10 Deep to My Day Ones

Let me take you back in time. There was a time when I was outside every weekend running the streets like I didn't have bills, responsibilities, or knees that would one day pop when I dropped down to get my eagle on (shout out to Nelly). I was rolling deep with a squad of 10 girls, yup, ten. We had matching outfits, inside jokes for days, and an energy that made every outing feel like a whole movie. We really thought we'd be friends forever, pulling up to each other's weddings, raising our kids like cousins, doing life side by side like it was guaranteed.

But life, yeah, she had other plans. Over time, that big loud ride-or-die crew started shrinking. Some friendships drifted.

Some exploded. And some just quietly faded away without warning, no beef, just distance. People grew, changed, and moved on. And so did I.

Now, my circle is small but mighty. I've got two real ones from high school who've stood the test of time and a few more I met along the way in adulthood. We've been through it all, heartbreaks, glow-ups, career pivots, and "Girl, am I crazy?" late-night convos. They've seen every version of me and never flinched. That's rare.

I used to feel bad when old friendships faded. I'd replay things in my head, wondering if I messed up or could've done more. But now I get it, not everyone's meant to stay. Some people are only in your life for a season or a lesson, and that's okay. Like they say, "Here for a good time, not a long time."

Because when you find your forever friends, the ones who love you loud, hold you accountable, and show up even when it's inconvenient, you realize it's never about how many people you have around you. It's about having the right ones. And I wouldn't trade these women for anyone else in the world. Period.

Self-Care = Self-Respect

Taking care of yourself isn't selfish; it's a form of self-respect. It's how you show up for yourself so you can actually show up in your life at school, at work, in relationships, and especially when no one's watching. And no, taking a break shouldn't require a breakdown as a prerequisite.

Adulthood isn't some sprint to the finish line. It's a long, winding journey with ups, downs, plot twists, and "what the heck am I doing?" moments. Some days you'll feel on top of the world, and other days it'll take everything just to get out of bed, and both are valid. That doesn't mean you're failing; it means you're human.

The key is having the right tools, consistent routines, and solid support systems in place. That's what helps you stay grounded when life gets messy, not perfection, not hustle, not pretending everything's fine. Real self-care is what keeps you stable when the storm hits, not just when the sun is out.

So give yourself permission to rest, reset, and take care of yourself, not when you've hit rock bottom, but before you even get close. That's not a weakness. That's wisdom.

Final Word: Because "Doing the Most" Won't Heal You

Start small with your self-care routine, like baby steps small. Try adding one self-care habit to your day and actually protect it like your peace depends on it, because it does. You don't need a fancy plan, a Pinterest-perfect morning routine, or all the answers. What you do need is a little space carved out just for you, where your needs matter, your breath slows down, and your nervous system can finally chill.

So focus on nurturing yourself every day. Breathe. Stretch. Journal. Nap without guilt. Say no without a dissertation. Reconnect with yourself without waiting for a meltdown to make it urgent. Because being well is the real glow-up, and you deserve to feel good without earning it through burnout.

About the Author

Christa Pierce is a proud mother, seasoned professional, and now author based in Maryland. With over four decades of experience navigating the challenges of parenthood, career growth, and personal development, she brings a wealth of real-life knowledge and hard-earned wisdom to her writing.

Christa holds a Bachelor's Degree in Communications from Georgia State University and a Master's Degree in Marketing from the University of Maryland Global Campus. With a background in tech, along with experience in communications and marketing, Christa brings a unique blend of creativity, strategy, and real-life wisdom to the table. Her passion for helping young adults navigate the real world is rooted in both her professional skillset and her personal journey of figuring things out the hard way. Now, she's using that knowledge to help others avoid the pitfalls and feel more prepared for life after moving out on their own.

Christa decided to turn her insights into a practical guide not just for her 23-year-old daughter, Tyler, but for young adults everywhere facing the often overwhelming transition into adulthood. Adulting 101: Things I Wish I Knew Before I Moved Out My Momma's House is her way of offering the kind of guidance she wishes she'd had, blending relatable stories with real-world advice to help the next generation navigate life with confidence.

www.ingramcontent.com/pod-product-compliance
Lightning Source LLC
Chambersburg PA
CBHW021639120626
46545CB00002B/617

*9 7 9 8 9 9 9 6 8 2 0 0 0 *